Harvesting for Eternity

Harvesting for Eternity

*A Common Man With An
Uncommon Faith*

Jerry Crane

Copyright © 2009 by Jerry Crane.

Library of Congress Control Number: 2009906382
ISBN: Hardcover   978-1-4415-5000-2
             Softcover   978-1-4415-4999-0

All rights reserved. No part of this book may be reproduced or transmitted in any form or by any means, electronic or mechanical, including photocopying, recording, or by any information storage and retrieval system, without permission in writing from the copyright owner.

This book was printed in the United States of America.

To order additional copies of this book, contact:
Xlibris Corporation
1-888-795-4274
www.Xlibris.com
Orders@Xlibris.com

Contents

Part I
Church Services 17

Part II
Organizational Meetings 91

Part III
Prison Ministry and Retreats 133

Part IV
School and Community Events 179

Part V
Dedication of Camp Griesheim Christian Retreat Center 209

Part VI
Weddings 215

Part VII
Funerals 231

Part VIII
Letters to Friends 275

Part IX
Jerry's Funeral 281

Part X
Epilogue 289

It is with deep gratitude that I would like to thank Carol Reiners. This book would not have come to pass without Carol's sorting and typing Jerry's notes, and then putting all of the pieces together. Thank you, Carol. May God bless you for the long hours you have put in and for the kindness and love you have shown to me and to Jerry.

Vicki Crane

This book is dedicated *"to the glory of God so that the Son of God may be glorified through it."* John 11:4

Altar built by Jerry Crane at Camp Griesheim
Christian Retreat Center

Biography

Jerry was a farmer in Central Illinois. He and his wife, Vicki, had four children: Todd, Tim, Tonya, and Tasha. Many years ago, Jerry attended a weekend retreat called Kogudus—a retreat about faith and life. Following the retreat, he was so inspired that he became involved in many similar retreats in Illinois and ten other states. He and Vicki traveled to the country of Estonia to help lead a retreat there. Jerry was also dedicated to reaching out to people in prison and led retreats in nine prisons in Illinois, two in Wisconsin, and one in Montana.

Also, after attending Kogudus, Jerry led a group of volunteers in creating a permanent Christian retreat center at a campsite east of Hartsburg. Having grown up in the area, the setting was near and dear to his heart. He and others completely renovated the existing building and also built an A-frame chapel to create Camp Griesheim Christian Retreat Center, thus fulfilling his dream of creating a place for worship and fellowship in a serene setting.

Jerry was active in his church and community. He taught Sunday school, served on the church council and chaired various committees in his church. He served on the elevator board for thirty-eight years, and also on the school board.

In 2004, Jerry and his wife, Vicki, traveled as part of the Gandhi Peace Delegation to the Holy Land. Arun Gandhi, Mahatma Gandhi's grandson, led the delegation along with official representatives from the Lutheran, Presbyterian, and Roman Catholic churches. The delegates met with key leaders from the Jewish, Christian, and Muslim faiths, including Yassar Arafat, as well as the common people of the land. Jerry touched many people in the Holy Land, but he especially touched the simple Palestinian farmers as he felt compassion for their great losses of land and crop. Jerry understood that God's way of living usually contradicts the world . . . usually contradicts our way. (More information about this trip is found in "Blessed by God," page 83.)

Jerry died in 2006, but he left behind a legacy. This book is a compilation of the many talks Jerry gave throughout his lifetime.

Quotes and Comments by Friends and Acquaintances

―――――ⱳ∽ჿჄჄჄჄჿ∾ⱳ―――――

In Chuck Colson's book, *Life Sentence*, Colson talks about a young man who was an alcoholic, had served time in prison, and while threatening suicide on the edge of a bridge, accidentally fell off the bridge and was never found. Chuck was wondering what he could have done differently. In his book he recalled meeting Jerry.

"Then I remembered Jerry, a young man in a lumberman's jacket, who stood up near the end of a prison fellowship meeting in Peoria, Illinois. Jerry reported that he had been visiting prisoners in the prisons for three years. He befriended a young Christian inmate, assuring him that, as his brother, he'd stand with him anywhere. Months later, the inmate was released and turned up on Jerry's doorstep. Jerry took the young man in, bought him a suit of new clothes, gave him a bed, and stuffed him with home-cooked food. The man stayed for several weeks, eventually getting a job, and then his own apartment.

"Jerry seemed pleased with himself as he told the story that day in Peoria. He put his index finger to his tongue and then chalked up number one on an imaginary blackboard. One success, he seemed to be saying. Everyone in the room smiled. Without changing his expression, Jerry then told how the man was arrested eight months later and was now back in jail. Jerry then made a quick erasing motion over the spot where seconds earlier he had marked the number one.

"'So,' he said, putting his hands in his pockets and shrugging his shoulders, 'I'm back to zero, but I'm still going into the prisons because that's where God wants me to be' . . ."

"Why would I remember Jerry now? I had been to a hundred or more meetings just like that one. Yet Jerry's face and his story were as vivid in my mind's eye as if he were standing before me in my office telling it all over again. Was it his honesty? He was surely honest, painfully so, confessing his own weakness.

"[I thought] anything done in the name of Christ must produce positive results. That's what other Christians and the world expect. To admit that this doesn't always work would be like saying that God's word isn't true or we are not really spiritual enough to draw on God's power . . .

"What is the answer? In a rare moment of awareness I saw it—the frank acknowledgment of our nothingness and total dependence on Jesus Christ, the search for truth, not through ourselves, but through Him and obtaining strength for service through the indwelling power of his Holy Spirit. **Jerry put it well: we do what we do out of obedience to Jesus.**

—Colson, Charles W., *Life Sentence* (Tarrytown, NY: Fleming H. Revell, 1979), pp. 289-291. Used by permission of the author

"Jerry Crane was a man who was really alive in the true sense of living. I introduced him at one retreat as a man who wore a lot of different shoes. He wore cowboy boots, sneakers, work shoes, and dress shoes according to where God was leading him. He touched a lot of people that have in turn touched the lives of others. Jerry's passion was that all people should know that God loved them and this was why the Kogudus Retreats were in prisons in Illinois. He did a talk about his son's death and the feelings that he had at the time and God's peace that he was now experiencing. The prisoners were quiet and you could tell they were focused on what he was communicating. Jerry played and sang the song, "Does Anybody Here Want to Live Forever," and there were tears all around. He was a man after God's own heart. He knew that he always needed God's help and that was Jerry's big strength."

—Ralph Ward, Correctional Chaplain II, retired
(Served at Hillsboro and Vandalia Correctional Centers in Illinois)

"He was not a one-dimensional person. When there was a difference of opinion, he would try to see both sides of it. He got along with everyone, and I mean everyone."

—Carl Hobbs, friend

"Crane was conscientious and sensible in all areas, including business. He was very good. He would understand a problem and help you choose the best path."

—Jeff Duckworth, general manager of Hartsburg Grain

"Jerry was my adoptive father and mentor, and there was no other man who knew Jesus on such a personal level. No other man who said, 'Use me, Lord. What can I do for you today, my king?' I am indebted to Jerry and his entire family, Todd, Tim, Tonya, and Tasha, for my life and for my very own wonderful family."

—Bob Eeten, friend

"There was a helpmate to hold, a family to raise, a farm to run, a camp to build, teams to train, retreatants to welcome, neighbors to serve. Jerry approached these assignments with care, steadiness, wisdom, humility, humor, hopefulness, and an implicit invitation to respond in kind. Thus communion was felt and community formed on the spot. Everyone who crossed his path has stories to tell of the encounter. The secret about Jerry, as for Paul and all who are his, is that Christ is in you. Thus it was often not Jerry we saw so much as Jesus. The hope of glory shone through Jerry with uncommon transparency."

—Pastor Gene Peisker

"Jerry Crane had thousands of friends because he took time to listen and talk with everyone the Lord put in his path. He made you feel important and loved, both by God and himself. Someone once said, 'Jerry would be as comfortable talking with the pope as he would a prisoner.'"

—Carol Reiners, friend

"One might wonder what Jerry would have said if he could have spoken at his own funeral. Of course, he would have said something funny. But I think he would have said in some fashion to each of us, 'Be a better person, be the best you can be.'"

—Rich Crane, brother

Foreword

Where Is God?

- Have you ever wondered what God has to do with your life Monday through Saturday?
- Do you feel like you are too ordinary for God to use you to impact other people's lives?
- Do you wonder where God is when your prayers aren't answered like you want?
- Where is God when a loved one gets sick or dies?
- Is he with you when you are working?
- When your life is going great and you're having fun . . . is God there too?

Many years ago, my husband Jerry and I attended a retreat on faith and life called Kogudus. Even though we had both attended church all of our lives, at that retreat, it all became real for us and we realized God has everything to do with our life Monday through Saturday—when we are sick, when we are working, when our prayers aren't answered like we want, when we lose loved ones, and when life is going great. A short time after that retreat, we dedicated our lives to Christ, as well as the lives of our four children.

When our son, Tim, died five years later, the attitude Jerry and I had was, what is God saying to us? What is he wanting us to learn from this? And that is the attitude we continued to have toward our problems and difficulties throughout the coming years.

In 2005 I suffered a brain aneurysm. It was sudden, I had no warning signs. Jerry later quoted the emergency room doctor as saying, "Your wife has blood on both sides of her brain and all across the front. I have to tell you, she cannot survive this." Miraculously, I survived. Four and a half months later, I was with Jerry when he died suddenly while undergoing a test in preparation for knee surgery. Then, seven weeks later, my mom died unexpectedly while I was standing at her bedside just a few minutes after we had been talking.

In all of this I have learned that God is sufficient. He is able to get us through things we would never have believed we could endure, and I believe the key is our attitude. It is easy to feel sorry for ourselves; it is something we have all done. Learning from our experiences is a much more difficult way; however, it is worth the effort and struggle. God has much to teach us when we are ready to listen.

This book is a collection of talks written by my husband, Jerry, a farmer—a common man with an uncommon faith—who recognized God in all things and at all times. They reveal his love for God, for his family, for his friends, and for others. He truly cared, it was real, and I was blessed to be his wife.

It is my prayer that as you read Jerry's book, it will help you think about God in your life during times of trial and tragedy, success and happiness, hopes and dreams. May God bless you.

Vicki Crane

Part I

Church Services

1. "Jesus Christ Superstar"—St. Peter's Lutheran Church, Emden, IL, October 14, 1973 19
2. "Our Mission"—Bartonville, IL, November 23, 1975 21
3. "Here I Stand"—St. Peter's Lutheran Church, Emden, IL 25
4. "The Ground Is Level at the Foot of the Cross"— St. Peter's Lutheran Church, Emden, IL 1983 27
5. "The Name of Jesus"—St. Peter's Lutheran Church, Emden, IL, January 1, 1986 31
6. "Where Is Our Treasure?"—Prince of Peace Congregation 37
7. "A Mountaintop Experience"—Gibson City, IL, March 1, 1987 41
8. "Amazing Grace"—St. Peter's Lutheran Church, Emden, IL, October 11, 1987 49
9. "When God Doesn't Bless Us Like We Ask"—Chillicothe, IL, August 7, 1988 55
10. "Showing Kindness to Our Neighbor"—St. Peter's Lutheran Church, Emden, IL, July 9, 1989 59

11. "Touched by God's Spirit"—St. Peter's Lutheran Church, Emden, IL, April 14, 1991 65
12. "Sow a Few Mustard Seeds"—St. Peter's Lutheran Church, Emden, IL, June 16, 1991..69
13. "The Gospel, St. Peter's, and Us"—St. Peter's Lutheran Church, Emden, IL, 1997...73
14. "Move Our Fence?"—Delavan Presbyterian Church, Delavan, IL, January 9, 2005 77
15. "Blessed by God"—St. John's Lutheran Church, Hartsburg, IL, January 20, 2005 83
16. "Born Again"—St. Peter's Lutheran Church, Emden, IL, April 10, 2005 87

1

"Jesus Christ Superstar"

St. Peter's Lutheran Church, Emden, IL

Laymen's Sunday, October 14, 1973

"Jesus Christ Superstar, are you really who you say you are?" is a line from a rock opera that was popular a couple of years ago. It has since been made into a movie. Why should a question such as this come from a musical play? Why have people been asking this question for almost two thousand years? Who was this man who, according to Christians, came and died so men may live forever?

Christians say he was the Promised One, the Prince of Peace, the Messiah, the Son of God—and he still lives. We call ourselves Christians because we have looked and searched and can find no other logical answer as to who Jesus is. If we are Christians, what does this mean to us? What does this mean to our community and those around us?

Some members of St. Peter's attended a Living Witness Institute at Emmanuel Lutheran Church in Minonk in which they visited homes.

Alice Lessen and Mary Heineken, along with a man from Minonk, went to a home and talked to a lady from that town. The man from Minonk knew this lady and her family and told Alice and Mary, "Let's not go there. She and her family attend church every Sunday. She and her husband each have relatives who are ministers. I know she has the assurance of heaven." But they went anyway because they wanted to share their faith and visit with her about the Living Witness Institute.

Mary asked the question, "If you die tonight and stand before God, and he were to ask you, 'Why should I let you into my heaven?' what would your answer be?" It became quiet. The woman couldn't answer. I believe there are literally thousands of people in our Christian churches who do not yet have the assurance of salvation.

How about each one of us? If we were to die tonight and stand before God, and he were to ask us, "Why should I let you into my heaven?" what would your answer be? If we can answer this question, we are on our way. The whole thing about being a Christian then makes sense. And if you can answer, what about your wife or husband? What about your son or daughter, mother, father, or friends and neighbors?

A new committee has been started in our church. It's called an evangelism committee. This fall there will be six-week study courses for people of every age, and hopefully, by February or March, a house-to-house visitation of every member of St. Peter's will be started. Think of it! Not 2 percent, but 100 percent of our congregation talking about Jesus Christ!

God said that Jesus is his Beloved Son with whom he is well pleased. Jesus said, "*Behold, I stand at the door and knock.*" It's like we are on the inside and Jesus is outside the door, but there is only one doorknob, and it's on the inside. Only we can open the door.

We have a job to do. It's a big job, but certainly not an impossible one. We just have to share what we have. "Jesus Christ Superstar, are you really who you say you are?" He said, "*I came that you might have life and have it abundantly.*" We're rich in the blessings of eternal life with him.

Amen.

2

"Our Mission"

Bartonville, Illinois

November 23, 1975

Good morning. My name is Jerry Crane, and I attend St. Peter's Lutheran Church in Emden, Illinois. It's good to be here. Good to come and worship with you. Maybe before we get started this morning we could pray together.

Lord, we praise you for this day, and we thank you that your Holy Spirit calls, gathers, and enlightens us. Now let the words that I say and the meditations of our minds and our hearts be acceptable, Lord, in your sight, our Strength and our Redeemer. Amen.

The theme given to me this morning, this Layman's Sunday, is called "Our Mission," and I would like very much to visit with you about this and how I think it fits together with the Gospel for today, which is one of the really great passages in the Bible. It's a picture of how common kindness—yes, common kindness—will affect our standing in the eternal world.

It was just read to you earlier, but since we are going to be thinking about it for the next few minutes, let's read it again, and try to picture the scene in our minds. It's talking about something important. Jesus is talking about his second coming and what to expect. This is the same Jesus who once said in Matthew 12, *"He who is not with me is against me, and he who does not gather with me, scatters."*

Now as we gather these thoughts in our mind, it is not the important thing to know exactly how Jesus' second coming will be. There is much speculation and difference of opinion on this, and it is best not to cloud our minds with a detailed theory as to exactly what is going to happen when he comes. We may be disappointed; many people were when he came the first time. They expected something entirely different. We aren't concerned about *how* he is coming. We know he *is* and that's what matters.

Now how or why should this tie into "our mission?" When we talk about our mission, we need to get a little more personal. When we talk about our mission, we think of our mission in and with the church, and rightly so; but it's too easy when we talk of our mission to kind of skim over our own life and just blend it in with a group. Every church needs to become more and more of a caring, sharing community. This is the goal of the church. But this goal can never be obtained without a personal commitment from each one of us. So more important than "our mission" is "my mission." Not "our mission," but "my mission," yours and mine.

Now when we think of my mission, that's where it starts to get personal. That's when it starts to take on meaning for each one of our individual lives. And it's at this point we must consider saying yes daily to Jesus Christ. I don't mean yes, you are God, or yes, Jesus, you are my Savior. I'm going to assume you have already made this commitment somewhere in your life. The yes to Jesus I'm referring to is the yes to the call to serve. "Yes, Jesus, what will you have me do?" There is almost no way you and I will ever know what our own personal mission is unless we daily say yes to the call to serve our fellow man because by serving our fellow man in and through Christ, what are we doing? Remember the Gospel? Jesus said, *"I was hungry, and you gave me food; thirsty and you gave me drink . . ."* How can we know what "my mission" is? What does Jesus want from me, and also, what do I want to do for him?

One of the ways we must consider as we think about "my mission" is daily Bible reading. If we are working for someone and really trying to do a good job, we report in first thing every morning to find out what he or she has to say. We need to report to the Lord first thing every morning. Our Lord speaks to us through the scriptures. Every problem we have has an answer if we turn it over to him. God's word in the scriptures has meaning for "my mission." We need to feed ourselves every day with God's word.

If we could live the perfect life, we wouldn't have to read every day, but we are real people. We are out in the business world and the "matters of the world." Worldly ideas try and take us over. The world feeds us daily with greed and ambition and corruption, and if that's all we get every day, it will soon take us over. And no matter how much we think we love the Lord, if we don't read and worship daily, we are in great danger of becoming separated from him.

Jesus himself says in John 15, *"If anyone separates from me, he is thrown away like a useless branch, withers, and is gathered into a pile with all the others [that's those who are of the world] and burned."* I think that the most important thing we as lay people need to do is to daily read God's word and commit ourselves to saying yes. Yes to the call to serve, and then serve in whatever capacity he may direct and lead us.

We need to learn to depend on Jesus, to trust him, to know him better. You know, if we don't trust someone completely, it's probably because we don't know him well enough. Get to know him better. He wants us to. He hung by nails for over six hours to prove it. For what? For recognition as a man or even as a God? No. He did it so people could see him as the Lord who cares, as the Lord who says, *"I love you. Come and serve your fellow man."*

"It may be too much," we say. "I don't want to know what he wants me to do. I don't want him to ask me." He already has. He asked each one of us when he committed himself to the cross. But you know what the fantastic thing about this is? That he even wants us to help him. He is so strong and we are so weak, yet he wants us to help him.

Christ is counting on us, you and me, to do our mission, "my mission" and "your mission." But as much as he counts on us, as much as he wants us to come to him and serve him by serving others, He will not force himself upon us. He will not go where he isn't welcome. I think he proved this when he came into the world. Mary and Joseph went to the inn, but there was no room in the inn, so they went to the stable. They were welcome there.

What is your mission, you as lay people? I don't know, but I do know this: people need Jesus. He is their only hope, and the world's full of those who don't know that. You can't save the world; God doesn't expect you to. But he does have something for each one of you to do, and he will give you the wisdom and the strength to do it. He will never ask you to do anything you aren't capable of doing. What he has for you to do is special because in his eyes, *you* are special, special enough that he died for you, each one of you.

Read his word daily, visit with him, worship him. Find "your personal mission" so when he, the Messiah, comes in his glory and all the angels with him, and when he sits upon the throne of glory and all of us are gathered before him, he will say to us on his right, *"Come—come, blessed of my Father, into the Kingdom I have prepared before you, for I was hungry and you fed me; I was thirsty, and you gave me water; I was a stranger, and you invited me into your house; naked, and you clothed me; sick and in prison, and you visited me. Yes, come, for when you did it to the least of these my brethren, you were doing it to me."*

3

"Here I Stand"

St. Peter's Lutheran Church, Emden, IL

Confirmation

It is said that the most knowledgeable people are those who have read what even more knowledgeable people have written. What's that mean? I guess it means most everyone's great ideas are all secondhand. They have come from someone else. Now that can be good. We need to know what others have found to be true. We need to read about things that are right and wrong, but I believe we mustn't let anyone else do our thinking for us. We mustn't let others push and pull us wherever they want whenever they will. There comes a time when we need to say, "Here I stand!"

Martin Luther seems to have been such a man. Sometimes, I think, in the Lutheran Church we have a tendency to raise Martin Luther up too high—yet other times I think we don't raise him up high enough, especially his message and his courage. Sure, he was just a man, but there was something about him. Something that made him say, "Here I stand."

You know, I believe there's only one way we can say, "Here I stand." That's if we know in our hearts what we believe. There's no changing it. *Here I stand.* We don't necessarily have to be able to prove it, yet we know it's true. By faith, here I stand. How can we be so sure? What do we need to be so sure?

Confirmation kind of goes along with commencement, and to commence means to begin. A lot of things you now know are what someone else you respect has told you. You know they are honest and trustworthy so you believe them—your parents, Pastor and Mrs. Spenn, your teachers. But now confirmation . . . to me it turns you loose to become what God intended for you to become, to go forward learning on your own—many times falling—yet running on to see what you are going to become. You're no longer little girls and little boys. You're young men and young women. You study, you read what others have written, you pray—a lot—and think—and you say, "I don't understand everything, but this I know: Jesus loves me. He forgives me. He died for me. Here I stand."

Continue your Christian education. Where is that? It's in your heart. How does it get there? By what you put into it. Your heart contains everything about you. You have a new heart. You got it when you accepted Jesus or, for most of you, when you were baptized. Now you're getting ready to renew those baptismal vows that others made for you. And with your new heart, you're ready to go. This is the beginning. Don't let it be the end. It's just the beginning.

Keep putting into your heart what you have prayed about, and what you feel is important. Tuck something away in there every chance you get. From the Bible—study it; from your thoughts and feelings—test them out and see if they are from God. From others who are studying also—like in Sunday school and from sermons. You may not agree with every sermon, but if God's word, his message of salvation is there, take something from it and stuff it into your heart, and you'll be able to say, "Here I stand. I know it is true; I cannot falter or sway; I believe it. Here I stand."

4

"The Ground Is Level at the Foot of the Cross"

St. Peter's Lutheran Church, Emden, IL

Pastor Appreciation Sunday—1983

This is Pastor Appreciation Month. We've been blessed here at St. Peter's by many fine pastors who have said yes to the call to serve Jesus and have come to live among us. In 1973 Pastor and Mrs. Spenn said yes to that call and moved in next door to the church.

The first meeting I attended with Pastor Spenn was a Sunday school teachers' meeting. I remember opening the meeting and right away, Pastor Spenn started edging forward in his chair. He had so many ideas and so much excitement, and he had so much knowledge that very quickly, he was in charge. And I remember thinking, "I'm not needed here."

It wasn't too long after, it seemed to me, that Pastor started to change. I asked him about it once, and he said, "I used to want to be in charge. I felt it was my job. And when a layperson was doing something that wasn't exactly right, I would correct him or her and make sure all the words were pronounced right and the facts were exactly right. But you know," he said, "the main thing is that the layperson is willing and that he knows Jesus Christ crucified. That's what's important. The ground is level at the foot of the cross," he used to say. "Everyone needs a Savior. Remember Ephesians 2:8 and 9: *'For by grace you have been saved through faith; and this is not your own doing, it is the gift of God—not because of works, lest any man should boast.'*" This was his favorite scripture passage.

Remember, one Sunday morning his light on the pulpit wouldn't work, and he was preaching and he was so excited he pounded on the pulpit to make a point, and the light came on? And remember, if you had a kid in confirmation and they didn't have their lesson done, it wasn't the kid who was in trouble, it was the parents. Confirmation was so important to Pastor and Leah. I remember once there was a discipline problem and Pastor and Leah called in us parents and they said, "We need your help," and I remember Leah cried. It was so important to them.

I could go on and on about this couple who said yes to the call to serve, but time doesn't allow it. One more. You remember the story he told about the lady who went to the beauty parlor and had her hair done, and afterward she looked in the mirror and was infuriated when she saw how she looked, and she said "I want justice!" And the beautician looked at her and said, "You don't want justice—you need mercy." And Pastor would hammer home God's grace and God's mercy that was already taken care of because Jesus died for us.

When Pastor Spenn was in the hospital, I went to see him. He had his Bible on the table next to his bed. He was feeling pretty good that evening and I remember thinking, "I want to know what he's thinking." He was always visiting the sick and now he's not well. I took his Bible and laid it next to him and said, "Read to me, Pastor." And this great authoritative person who liked to be in charge slid the Bible back across his bed and said, "You read to me, Jerry." I can't remember to this day what

I read. I guess it doesn't matter. What matters is he placed the scripture in a layman's hand. He knew it wouldn't be perfect. He knew I wouldn't pronounce all the words right, but he wanted me to read to him.

Was Pastor Spenn perfect? No, but he had a perfect God. Did he have a perfect wife? Pretty close. It was a tremendous witness to us, Leah, when in your time of sorrow, you were able to celebrate Pastor's death by carrying on his and your work by finishing the confirmation class.

Leah, we cannot hear and see the Gospel without it changing us. Thank you for saying yes to the call to serve at St. Peter's.

5

"The Name of Jesus"

St. Peter's Lutheran Church, Emden, IL

January 1, 1986

The text for today is going to be the Gospel that Gary Marten just read for us from Luke 2:21, but before I read that again, Gary and I want to thank you for allowing us to be here this morning. I think Gary does a really good job with the liturgy and should consider continuing this type of work in the church. Gary and Gail are going to sing later on and we look forward to that.

A couple weeks ago, Tom and Lee Komnick and I went to hear the past secretary of Agriculture speak. He told a story about a pastor who was always able to keep his message short. He found out that the pastor's secret was to pop a cough drop into his mouth at the beginning of the sermon and when the cough drop was gone, he would conclude. This particular morning the pastor made a mistake and popped a button into his mouth. He said he finally left after a couple of hours, and as far as he knew, the pastor was still talking. I don't have any secrets so if this message gets too long, just do what he did, get up and leave.

The Gospel for today might seem a little confusing, because if you were here last Sunday, the Gospel was about Jesus in the temple at the age of twelve, and today the Gospel tells us about the naming of Jesus just eight days after his birth. So we're backing up today. Let me read today's Gospel once more—Luke 2:21.

On our church calendar, January 1 is called the "Name of Jesus," and is one of the festivals on the church calendar. This is the day we celebrate the naming of Jesus. You notice the scripture says he was named Jesus, the name the angel told Mary to give to the baby *before* he was conceived.

I'd like to go back this morning to that time when the angel, we are told his name was Gabriel, visited Mary. I'd like to go back those forty plus weeks before Jesus' official naming and see once more what led up to this time. That's the Christmas story, you say. We've heard that story a dozen times the last two weeks. I want to go back because, as I said, January 1 is the Name of Jesus festival in the church. It is also New Year's Day on our calendars that hang on our kitchen wall or that sit on our desk at home or work.

New Year's Day means many different things to us. Our minds jump forward and backward. We look back to the memories of the past and all that's happened before. We look back with gladness—and we look back with sadness. Carol Reiners looked up some statistics for me this week, and she found that here at St. Peter's, we had eighteen baptisms and eight weddings last year. The joy that comes from those occasions!

The year 1985 also brought eleven funerals to our church. Some of us in our church have buried children, some grandchildren. Some have buried their mate, some a parent or a brother or sister, all of us a friend—and no matter how complete our loved one's life may have been, no matter how happy we know they now are, the waves of sadness sometimes overtake us as we look back. For all of us who have been to the cemetery in the past year—or years—may God continue to uphold us and assure us of the blessed hope and knowledge of eternal life.

As we look ahead, we look forward to the new year and what it will bring. We look forward with joy and anticipation. Sometimes we look forward in fear—maybe over a sickness—maybe over our marriage—maybe fear over our farm or business. There are many things to fear.

One of the things we do, as we look forward to the new year, is make resolutions—New Year's resolutions. We do this to try and improve our life, to make it better and to help get rid of, or lose, our fears. I'm going to be a better husband or father—wife—mother. I'm going to go on a diet. I'm going to quit smoking. I'm going to be more careful how I spend money this year. I'm going to read the Bible more.

I said earlier that I want to go back this morning—back to where the angel visited Mary before he was conceived, back to where the angel Gabriel said, *"You shall name him Jesus."* I want to go back because something happened there, something we can look at and say, "That's for me." And it doesn't matter if you're a Billy Graham or a factory worker or a farmer, or unemployed, or sick or well. It's for you and it's for me.

Yes, it was the beginning of the Christmas story—the angel telling us that Jesus was going to be born to save us from our sins. But it was more than that. Something else happened, something we can take into our lives that I believe can be better than New Year's resolutions—something to help us with the sadness of the past and the fears of the future—something to give real meaning to the joys we've had and the joys we anticipate.

Let's go back to where the angel visited Mary—when the birth of Jesus was announced to her. Let me read a few verses from Luke 1: 26-36. Mary said, *"I am the handmaiden of the Lord."* The Living Bible, in words we might use today, says, *"I am the Lord's servant, and I am ready to do what He wants!"* Can we say that? I wonder, if we could say that, would it be better than New Year's resolutions? Could this help our lives more?

"I can't do that," we say. "I can't be expected to say what Mary said. Why, an angel came to her! I could do it if an angel came to me." The man who was named Jesus? I believe he—through the Holy Spirit—brings us the word of God today, as surely as the angel Gabriel brought the word of God to Mary. It comes through our Bibles, and our churches, and each other. This man named Jesus—he tells us we don't need an angel. He asks us to have faith.

Jesus says you must have faith. Blessed are those who do not see and yet believe. Remember Thomas? Some of the disciples had seen Jesus after the resurrection. They told Thomas, *"We have seen the Lord."*

Thomas said, *"Unless I see the scars from the nails, unless I put my fingers on those scars and place my hand into his side, I cannot believe."*

Several days later Jesus appeared to the disciples again, and this time Thomas was there. Jesus went to Thomas and said, *"Thomas, Thomas, put your fingers on the nail scars, place your hand in my side."*

Thomas said, *"My Lord and my God."*

Jesus said, *"Thomas, you believe because you have seen. Blessed are those who do not see yet believe!"*

He's saying, I think, *"Blessed are those who have faith to believe my word,"* the word we hear from our Bibles, our church, and each other. What does all this mean this morning? I believe it means the word of God came to Mary and she said, *"I will do whatever you want."* She made a new commitment to God and God gave her the strength to carry it out.

Maybe that's what we need as we look back and forward this New Year's Day—a new or refreshed commitment. Maybe if we could get to know this man with the name of Jesus a little better, our fears would be eased. We would know that even if we couldn't see or feel it, our sorrows would have meaning and purpose—and our joys would be complete. Yet, we have so many things to think about. Our lives are already crowded with too many commitments. Do we have room in our hearts for this kind of commitment?

Some of you were at the cantata here the Sunday before Christmas. The first song was entitled, "Come to My Heart, Lord Jesus." Maybe that could be our prayer as we start out 1986. Gary and Gail are going to sing that song now and then we will conclude.

And he was called Jesus, the name given by the angel before he was conceived. Believe me, I know it's not easy. I have fears for 1986. My business is not what I would like it to be. I worry about my family. I have past sorrows that are not yet healed. But on this day, January 1, 1986, the day called the Name of Jesus in our church, I know that if we keep that name ever present in our minds and our hearts, all things will work together for our good according to his purpose.

May each of us remember that name, and may each of us have a blessed 1986. Amen.

6

"Where Is Our Treasure?"

Prince of Peace, 1986

Where is our treasure? The Gospel lessons have been taken from Luke for several Sundays now, and I notice they are going to continue. Luke seems to be lovingly telling us about Christ's ministry here on earth, and God's forgiveness; yet he also seems to be warning us. We don't like warnings. They make us feel uncomfortable, and no one likes to feel uncomfortable.

I'm a farmer. My son and I have forty-five thousand bushels of old corn sealed with a government loan for $2.58 per bushel. With interest about $2.75, it's worth $1.50. What do I do? What can I do? I know, I'll let the government take it. They'll take it over, call the loan square, no questions asked. They can't take it. Logan County has no place to go with it. What can I do? I'll take it to the elevator. The elevator is full and can't get shipping orders. I know, I'll store the old corn. The government will pay 26.5¢ storage, and I'll sell the new crop. New crop corn is 50¢ to $1.00 below cost of production. I can't make myself sell. I know, I'll tear down a hog barn I'm not using, build a new bin, and take out another government loan until the price goes up, and then I can sell.

All right, it took two weeks of solid planning, telephone calls, and trips to the ASC office where they handle the corn loans, but I have the solution: store it all. Store it in old bins, tear down the old barn, store it in new bins, in barns, and everywhere else I can. I did it! Now I can rest, secure the crops will be stored, and I can wait for the market to go up. It always does . . . sometime. And then the Gospel from Luke reads—but wait, that's not me! Those treasures aren't for me. They're for the banker and the landlord for cash rent and my family. I'm okay. But today Luke says, "*Where your treasure is, there will your heart be also.*"

What is my treasure? Is it what I think about most of the time, the farm or the business? I told Vicki the other day that it seems almost impossible to keep a business going without thinking about it constantly. Maybe it's not the business you think about all the time. Maybe it's your family, maybe your wife or husband, maybe someone else's wife or husband. Or is it Christ? Can any of us say that Christ is the number one thing in my life? He is my treasure. "*Seek ye first the kingdom of God and all these things will be added unto you.*"

What is your treasure? What do you spend more time thinking about than anything else? What makes your heart jump when you wake up in the morning?

I remember in 1957, my dad helped me buy a red 1956 Buick convertible. I got it on the Saturday afternoon of the state fair twenty-nine years ago, about like yesterday. I filled it up in Emden, picked up Vicki for a ride, went home, and parked it in the crib. Sunday morning when I woke up, my heart jumped. I jumped into my pants and shoes, and with my shoestrings flopping, I ran to the crib and looked at my car. Boy, was it a treasure!

Where is that car today? I don't know, probably melted down inside another car or maybe a refrigerator, gone forever. God is still here. The promises of Christ are still here. Maybe that's getting a little carried away. We say, of course, God is here. Of course, God has always been here. I know that, and he knows that I know that. He doesn't expect my heart to jump for joy when I think about him in the morning or forsake my business to think only of him or to not put my family first. That's foolish. When I get older, you know, real old, maybe then I might. *"For where your treasure is, there will your heart be also."* God looks at the heart.

In the fall of 1978, I was harvesting corn. I knew of a farm for sale, eighty acres. All day I tried to figure out a way to buy it. If I could get that farm, what a treasure I'd have.

That evening my two sons were coming to the field when they had a wreck. Todd was not hurt, but Tim was. Vicki came out, we called for an ambulance, and they took him to Lincoln, then to Springfield where they operated. He did everything the doctors said. He improved rapidly and was soon out of intensive care.

Basketball was Tim's treasure. He couldn't wait to play. However, he had a setback and was put back into intensive care. He said he prayed all night and thought he was going to die and go to heaven. The next night we lost him. The farm wasn't important anymore. Tim was a treasure, and he was gone. We had lost him. Nothing else seemed important, except the treasure of eternal life. Basketball didn't do it; I didn't do it. Only God. Tim didn't call for me. His treasure was in heaven. What he learned in Sunday school and confirmation had moved from his mind to his heart.

My story is not greater or lesser than yours. Most of us are lay people, not trained, but we know the kindness of Christ. We have a treasure. 1 Peter 2:9-10 says, *"You are a chosen people, God's priests, God's own people, called to proclaim the wonderful acts of God. Once you were no people; you didn't even know mercy. Now you have received it."* Yes, we are just lay people, untrained. But what a treasure!

I believe with all my heart that God, through Christ, has provided a way that we can put him first and still be able to have our families and whatever else God feels we need. Christian people are citizens of heaven, sojourners here for a while, cumbered with daily earthly cares, but with their eyes ever fixed on heaven.

7

"A Mountaintop Experience"

Gibson City, Illinois

March 1, 1987

Good morning. I'm glad to be here to worship with you this morning. I guess if I were you and came to church this morning and found a farmer standing in the pulpit, I'd wonder what was happening.

My name is Jerry Crane, and I do farm near Hartsburg. Hartsburg is located about halfway between Peoria and Springfield on Route 121. If you've ever driven from Morton to Lincoln on Route 121, you've gone right by our home.

I attend St. Peter's Lutheran Church in Emden where Frank Pieper is our pastor. Before him was Pastor Robert Spenn, whom some of you might remember. Vicki has attended church there all her life, and I have since our marriage. Our children all attended confirmation school there, and Vicki and I feel a real bond to the church and the community.

The book of Matthew was chosen this morning for the Gospel reading. I'd like to read it once more as we will be talking about this "mountaintop experience" Jesus shared with Peter, James, and John. We know this is an important passage because Mark and Luke also recorded the same account. (Read Matthew 17:1-9).

As I read it over this week, there were a couple of questions that came into my mind. The first was the six days. It starts by saying six days later. What happened six days before? When I looked this up in Mark, he also said *"six days later."*

I backed up a few verses and what I found was this: Jesus and his disciples were on their way to the territory near the town of Caesarea Philippi, and Jesus asked them, *"Who do people say that I am?"*

They answered, *"Some say John the Baptist, others say Elijah, some say Jeremiah, some say a prophet."* I don't know what Jesus did then, but I have a picture in my mind of him walking in front, and the disciples following, and I picture him coming to an abrupt halt and turning and looking them straight in the eye and saying, *"What about you? Who do you say that I am?"*

Jesus knew his time was short, and he wanted his disciples to know for sure what was going on. I don't know if there was a long silence or if Peter blurted it out, but Peter answered, *"You are the Messiah, the Son of the living God."*

As they went on down the road, Jesus began to tell them how he was to go to Jerusalem and suffer much, even be put to death, but he would rise from the dead three days later. He also told them how they must be willing to suffer if they wanted to follow him.

It seems as though these teachings were very important for the disciples, and they were fresh in Peter's and James' and John's minds when Jesus took them upon a lonely mountain six days later.

One of the other questions I had was with the word "transfiguration." What does that mean exactly? I knew it meant to change, but how? I looked in a Bible dictionary and it said, "Transfiguration: the name given to that singular event recorded in [then it gave reference to the gospel we read this morning] when Jesus was visibly glorified in the presence of three select disciples." The account portrays the transformation as outwardly visible and consisting in an actual physical change in the body of Jesus.

Luke says, *"The fashion of His countenance was altered."*

Matthew said, *"His face did shine like the sun."*

And Mark said, *"His garments became glistening, exceeding white."* In other words, whiter than white. It goes on to say the glory was not caused by the falling of a heavenly light on Jesus, but by the flashing forth of a radiant splendor within him. It was witnessed by Peter, James, and John and occurred while Jesus was praying. It said one other thing. It said the natural simplicity of the accounts and their sober insistence upon its detailed features powerfully testify to the reality of the event.

We know Peter never forgot it. He carried this memory with him, and later in II Peter 1:14-18 when Peter was contemplating his own death, he said, *"We have not made up stories to tell you about this Jesus. With our own eyes we saw His greatness. We were there on the mountain when He was given glory and honor by God, and we heard God say, 'This is my own dear Son with whom I am well pleased.' We heard it when we were there on the Holy Mountain."*

So what happened here? Jesus, while walking down a dusty road, turned to his disciples and said, *"Who do you say that I am?"*

Peter responded, *"You are the Christ, the Son of the living God."* Six days later he took Peter, James, and John up the mountain, and they witnessed his transfiguration in their presence. Moses and Elijah were there. God spoke to them.

Why? What's the bottom line here? I believe it was simply to get Peter to testify to who he thought Jesus was, and then to have their faith strengthened there on the mountain by what they witnessed. He did this by letting Peter, James, and John get to know him better and understand who he was. What is Jesus wanting of us here at the American Lutheran Church this morning? Probably the same thing. He asks us, "*Who do you say that I am? What do you believe?*" And then he urges us to get to know him better.

In 1973, I was invited to attend a Christian retreat supported by the Lutheran Church. It was called Kogudus. I didn't have the foggiest idea what it was, let alone what the word Kogudus meant. It started on a Friday evening with a steak dinner and ended Sunday afternoon after church. About twenty-five or thirty men gathered at a fraternity house in Urbana over semester break, and we stayed there for the whole weekend. We heard a talk about listening to God and listening to one another. We talked about our statement of faith. What did I believe? What did it mean when I said the Creed? As I thought about this question, I thought about what we read this morning when Jesus was walking with his disciples.

You see, sooner or later, Jesus is going to turn to us and say, "*Who do you say that I am?*" Or "*What do you believe?*" This question will probably not come from Christ himself. It will probably come through a friend or our child or a parent, but it will come. It may even come from the person looking back at you from your mirror. What do you believe? Or as Jesus said to his disciples, "*Who do you say that I am?*"

I guess that retreat called Kogudus doesn't sound like much, but it was a big deal for me. I left the retreat with a new appreciation of what Christ has done for me and a new appreciation for the church, God's body of believers, who, down through the years, has kept the message and the sacraments alive so I could hear it. The church, with all its differences, all its shortcomings, and all its prejudices, even with all these things going against it, God's people still united with Christ to preserve the message so all of us could hear it all these years. Isn't that something?

"Kogudus," by the way, I found out, was an Estonian word that meant "Christian fellowship." The reason it was called Kogudus was because the Lutheran pastor who started the retreat, Pastor Magis, was from Estonia and in fun wanted to get something in the retreat from his background, and the name stuck.

I also learned that his father was a Lutheran pastor in Estonia, and while Pastor Magis was studying for the ministry, war broke out in Estonia. They found themselves in the middle of the Nazi and Communist conflict, and as thousands of the Estonian people fled, he was captured and put into prison. He later escaped and was placed in a displaced persons' camp. While he was there, the church from America reached out and brought him and other refugees to America. He was able to finish his education and become a pastor. Because of this act of kindness from the church in America, Pastor Magis had a special reverence for the church. That was one reason the love for the church came out so much at Kogudus.

As I said earlier, this retreat meant a lot to me. Over the next few years, many people from our community attended a Kogudus. Over one hundred people have gone from our church. We have since built a retreat center in our area that we rent out to churches and Christian groups. We have roughly five or six Kogudus retreats per year. In the first ten years the retreat center was open, thirteen thousand people from all different churches all over the state of Illinois came to hold retreats.

What does all this have to do with the Gospel lesson this morning? It seems to me that Jesus took his disciples up on the mountain so they could get to know who he really was. You and I are here this morning to worship. Many of us have heard about Christ from the cradle on up. To be realistic, we will most likely never see anything like Jesus revealed to his disciples on the mountain. But what is really important is that we get to know Christ better and better. Sometimes that knowing comes to us through those around us and it especially comes to us through our churches.

Several years ago, Vicki and I were given the opportunity to really appreciate Christ coming to us through his people, the church. Our fourteen-year-old son, Tim, was badly injured in a van accident. He was taken to Lincoln and then on to Springfield, where he had an operation. He had to go seven days without food or water. People came to us, supported us with prayer, and stayed in the hospital with us.

He began to recover and people rejoiced with us, but suddenly he got worse. They decided to operate again. Pastor Spenn came with family and friends. We waited in the chapel while the doctor kept us posted. It was not going very well; it was very bad. Although we were concerned, we felt he would be okay. Then the doctor came in looking very grave. He said they had lost him. My son, voted most valuable player in basketball, was dead.

We asked if we could see him. They said, of course, he's your son. Vicki and I, and our other son, Todd, sat down in the room with him. As I sat there for a few minutes, Tim's short life of fourteen years swept through my mind. I felt very close to Christ and I wondered about the verse that said Christ will not give you more than you can stand. Maybe that's why he felt close—to watch over me, because I felt I couldn't stand much more. As I sat there, I felt in my mind, in my heart—I don't know—but I felt that Christ looked me in the eye and said, "*Who do you say that I am?*" I felt it was unfair. When Tim was so sick, I felt I turned his life over to him. I was counting on him. I was sure because of this Tim would be okay. Now he was dead.

Who do you say that I am? God's ways are not always our ways. He was and is who Peter said. *"You are the Christ, the Son of the living God."* He loves us all and died for us all, especially for Tim, and someday Tim's body, and mine and yours, will also be transfigured in some manner to go and be with Christ.

What happened up on that mountain, I'm not sure, but Peter was there and he never forgot it. He got to know Christ better than you or I probably ever will in this life, but just getting to know him better, that's what's important for us.

We talked about Kogudus this morning. It was a very important event in my life. It helped me to see all the things the church had been telling me all along. I heard nothing at Kogudus that the church hadn't already told me. It's just that setting aside the whole weekend, I was able to see it more clearly. In no way do I want to leave with you the impression that Kogudus is a must for salvation. It isn't, but it is a good way to get to know Christ better. It is no substitute for the church, but it helps strengthen what the church has been telling us for two thousand years.

We are about to enter into Lent. Lent is like spring or like a seed put in the ground. We start with Ash Wednesday and move toward the cross. It is a dark and cold place to be, like a seed in the ground. It's a time of repentance, and a time to get to know Christ better. After the cross comes the resurrection, a new life, like the seed coming out of the ground. It's spring, and everything is new.

Christ died for us all. Lent can be that "mountain of transfiguration" for us. Sometime before you go to bed tonight, look in the mirror and ask that person there, "Who do you say that Jesus is?" Amen.

8

"Amazing Grace"

St. Peter's Lutheran Church, Emden, IL

Laity Sunday, October 11, 1987

The text for today is the gospel from Matthew that Leonard Krusemark just read. I'd like to read it once more before we begin. (Matthew 20:1ff) Lord, please let the words that are spoken here this morning be your words. Amen.

"*Jesus said to them,*" the Gospel begins. Who was Jesus talking to here? If we back up a little in Matthew, we can see that Jesus is talking to his disciples about the kingdom of heaven. Jesus had been with the crowds teaching and they had brought the children to him so he could bless them. After that he left the crowds to be with his disciples.

A rich young Jewish man came to where they were and asked Jesus, "*What must I do to inherit eternal life?*"

Jesus said, "*Keep the commandments.*" "*Which one?*" the young man asked. Jesus said, "*Do not kill, do not commit adultery, do not steal, do not *accuse anyone falsely, respect your father and mother."* Jesus went on to say, *"Love your neighbor as yourself." "I have obeyed all these,"* the man said. He obviously felt sure that he had.

Jesus looked at him with love in his heart and said, *"If you really want to love your neighbor as yourself, go—sell all you have and give the money to the poor."* The rich young man's face fell, because he was very rich—and he walked away.

Jesus told his disciples how hard it was for a rich man to get into heaven. The disciples were amazed at this, and they asked Jesus, *"Well, how can anyone be saved?"* Jesus said it's impossible for men, but with God *all* things are possible. Peter spoke up and said, *"Lord, we gave up everything for you. What reward will we get?"* It was in answer to this question that Jesus told the parable of the workers in the vineyard that is our gospel for today.

Before he started the story, and again at the end, Jesus said, *"Many who are first will be last, and many who are now last will be first."* Now I'm not a theologian, I'm a farmer. I have worked for others, and sometimes others have worked for me. It never did make sense to me that those who worked all day until dark, picking and sorting grapes in the hot sun—maybe under the pressure of an approaching storm—should receive no more pay than those who worked for just an hour. That isn't the way a farmer would do it. It probably isn't the way a union man would do it either. The world sure wouldn't agree with this policy. But Jesus' ways are not our ways.

Remember the Old Testament reading Leonard read from Isaiah? *"My thoughts are not your thoughts, and my ways are not your ways,"* said the Lord. Jesus told the rich young man, *"Love your neighbor as you love yourself."* How do we do that? I believe to really do this we need to look at our neighbor from our neighbor's point of view. Let me explain. We look at the parable of the workers in the vineyard through our point of view. I wouldn't work all day in the sun for the same wage as those who work only one hour. It's not fair. I deserve more!

Was it unfair? The owner of the vineyard went out early in the morning to hire workers. He went to the market where they gathered. He negotiated with those he chose and they settled on a denarius. Now a denarius was a small coin about the size of a dime, I'm told. It contained very little silver. In itself it wasn't worth much, but it purchased quite a bit in those days. A denarius was a day's wage. I read this week that a denarius was what a government soldier made per day. The owner of the vineyard and the workers settled on the average day's pay for a day's work.

Let's look at the parable through another point of view. Whenever we've heard this parable, have we ever asked ourselves about the men who went into the vineyard at the eleventh hour of the day? Those who went to work just before sundown? Let's think about those men. Why in the world were they sitting idle in the market place all day long during the busy grape harvest season? Why did they have to say, "*No man would hire us*"? Was it because they didn't care if they worked or not? Were they lazy? I don't think so. There was no unemployment. You either worked or begged or starved. They, I believe, wanted to work. They had to work.

Could it be that they were the older and maybe feebler men? Could it be that they had been sick, or they were just naturally not the strong workers? Surely these men, for whatever reason, were obviously unfit and could not be counted on to do a full day's work that was needed in the harvest season. The fittest and the strongest laborers were all chosen early in the morning—the least fit later on, but some men were obviously so unfit for any hard work that no sensible person could afford to take them if he wanted to get a good job done.

Picture yourself sitting there in the labor market all day long, during the busy season, needing desperately something to take home to your wife and children at the end of the day, but knowing you're just too old, or too weak to be able to earn even a half day's work. Think of the despair in the minds of those men, weaker and sicker than the rest, but with the same needs as those who were chosen earlier. Think how hopeless they must have felt as the hours passed, knowing at the end of the day there would be nothing for their loved ones. They had the same needs.

Think, if you can, what it must have meant to those men to find out just before sundown that they were given an hour's work—just like the other men—and then to receive a full day's pay to take home with them—maybe for the first time in weeks. Think how they felt as they walked through the door to their families with a full day's pay!

So, what kind of man was the owner of the vineyard? Was he a man who simply demanded a full day's work for a day's pay from his early hired employees, or was he a man who noticed the needs of all the men? You see, no one came out short. Those who worked all day received their rightful earnings. No one was wronged, but many received far more than they had actually earned. They received grace! For grace is giving to others not what they have earned; nor, according to the selfish desires of the strong fit men who deserved to receive more than they had rightfully earned, but grace gives according to need!

The true meaning of grace is summed up in the words of Jesus to the rich young man—*"Thou shalt love your neighbor as you love yourself."* That can be done by not only noticing needs, but by looking at those needs through the eyes of those who have them. We are all called to work in the vineyard. To work in the vineyard is a privilege and the pay is pure grace. To question that grace for others is to lose it for oneself.

I read a story once—a fable, where many Christian people were waiting to get into the gates of heaven. They had been standing there in the sun for a long time and they were getting impatient. Finally an angel shouted from behind them, "Please step aside—please make way, we need to get these people in first," and the angel parted the crowd and brought forth the slaves, the unfit, some prisoners, and the maimed. The crowd became angry and shouted, "We were here first. We've been waiting a long time. We served the church and did work for the kingdom. Why do these people get in first?" To question that grace for others is to lose it for oneself. And the fable goes on—at that instant those souls were lost!

This is laity Sunday, a Sunday set aside to encourage us all to love our neighbors as we love ourselves. If we feel that we are too old, or too weak, or we can't afford to take the time off work, or we don't know the Bible well enough—that's okay. Do what you can and what you are able. Jesus said the last shall be first and the first last. Like the workers in the vineyard, we will be paid according to our needs—not according to what we have earned! Isn't that tremendous? But that's the way God is. His ways are not our ways. We rejoice in that. Amen.

9

"When God Doesn't Bless Us Like We Ask"

Our Savior's Lutheran Church, Chillicothe, IL

August 7, 1988

Good morning. My name is Jerry Crane and I'm happy to be with you this morning. I want to thank Craig Berger for inviting me, and all of you for letting me come. I'm a farmer from Hartsburg, about halfway between Peoria and Springfield on Route 121. I started out the year hoping for a bumper crop, and now find myself in what climatologists tell me is the worst drought central Illinois has ever encountered.

I'd like to use the Gospel lesson this morning for the text. I know I need it and I hope you can benefit from it too. I'd like to read it again (John 6:24ff). Will you please join me in prayer? Lord, please bless our coming together here in your name. Help us to realize above all things that you are the Bread of Life. Amen.

This week as I read the Gospel for today, I needed to back up a little to see what has happened just prior to this event. There we find the feeding of the five thousand, a miraculous story—one that was so big an event that it's found in all four Gospels. You may have read or studied it last week, but I think I'd like, if you don't mind, to review it a little this morning.

Jesus had been preaching and teaching in the Galilee area. The Bible says that Jesus went to the other side of the Sea of Galilee or the Sea of Tiberius. If you ever had occasion to see a map of the Sea of Galilee, you might notice it is shaped somewhat like the state of Illinois, and Tiberius is on the left side of the map about midway down with Capernaum, near the top. These are the two geographic areas we'll be talking about this morning.

Of course, Jesus knew more about the people than they knew themselves. They thought they had everything figured out. Jesus was to be their king. He could produce food for the people and they wouldn't even have to work. What a king he would make! But Jesus said to them, *"You seek me, not because you saw signs, but because you ate your fill of the loaves."* The people said they believed because they saw the signs of Jesus, but Jesus said, *"You seek me only for what I gave you."*

I read the other day that a faith that feeds on signs is an appetite that grows by what it feeds on; it cannot rest in the revelation of the given sign, but demands another. Why were the people like that, or more importantly, why are we like that? We want to see a sign from Jesus—then we will believe. "Lord," we say, "give me food that I may believe," and we get food and we are happy and we feel blessed. God loves me. But when we get hungry, we again say, "Lord, give me food that I may believe." What if we don't get what we want? Do we no longer believe?

"Lord, bless me with a better job. Lord, bless me with a family that brings me honor. Lord, bless me with a nice house for the family you gave me. Lord, bless me with a better car. Lord, heal me. Lord, bless me with rain, my crops are dying." You may pray, "Lord, bless us with a new and beautiful and glorious church that we may have a sign that we made the right decision here. Lord, give us this bread always."

What if there isn't another sign? Can we still love and trust Jesus? What if there is no rain? What if there is no new church? What if we are not healed? I'm not saying we shouldn't ask for these things, or that Jesus doesn't want us to have them. What I'm saying is, like the people crowded around Jesus at the Sea of Galilee, we say, "Lord, give us this bread always," always looking at the gift instead of the giver. But Jesus says, "*I am the Bread of Life. He who comes to me will not hunger and he who believes in me shall never thirst.*" It isn't the blessing or the sign—it's the Lord!

A few years ago during October, I was combining corn. Vicki brought our sons, Todd and Tim to the field. Todd was sixteen, Tim fourteen. They wanted to work after school. I told them to go to another farm about six miles away to plow. They took Vicki home and headed to the field in the van. About four miles down the road, they went off the road and then turned over in a field. When Vicki and I got there, Todd was walking around. He was okay, but Tim had been thrown through the windshield and the van had rolled over him. He was struggling to breathe. We were kneeling on the ground beside him, and Vicki said she kept hearing in her mind as she looked across the field, "*This is not unto death, but for the glory of God.*"

Five years prior to that time, Vicki and I had attended a Kogudus Retreat. This retreat is about renewal of your faith. After attending we said, "So this is what it is all about. Christ really did die for us and we really are saved if we accept him as our Lord and Savior." We had heard this in church all our lives, but when we went to Kogudus, we heard it for the first time. We became involved in the Kogudus program and ended up taking it to state prisons in Illinois, as well as other states. Through those experiences we ended up having two ex-offenders come to live with us at different times. We tried hard to listen to God and follow his leading. So, while Tim was lying there in the field, we felt through that verse, "*This is not unto death, but for the glory of God,*" he was telling us that Tim was not going to die.

The ambulance soon came and took him to Lincoln Hospital. In Lincoln, they sent him on to Springfield and took him into surgery. The surgery lasted six hours—he had a ruptured esophagus. After the surgery he couldn't eat or drink and couldn't talk because of the tube in his throat, but he kept his spirits up and was focused on his recovery because he wanted to get back to playing basketball.

A little over a week later, they moved him out of intensive care and he could whisper some words to us, but he soon had a setback and they took him back into intensive care. They were going to have to operate again. I went in to Tim and he whispered, "I've been praying all night. I think I'm going to die but I'm not afraid. I know I'm going to heaven." During his surgery, we stayed in the chapel and prayed with family and friends. Then the doctor came in and said, "We lost him."

We had a memorial service and our pastor let me give the message. It was for Tim's friends, and I told them what Tim had said and what he relied on when everything else failed: not friends, not basketball, not even me. He relied on Christ. This was not unto death. Tim is alive and he has gone on.

If Jesus blesses us with some bread—be thankful. But, if for some reason, he chooses not to, let us remember that he is the real bread of life—and if something that seems awful and traumatic happens to us or those we love, and we scream and cry, "I don't want it," there is a gift in there somewhere—and that gift is Jesus. That's the kind of Savior we have. Jesus said, "*I am the Bread of Life. He who comes to me shall not hunger and he who believes in me shall never thirst.*" Amen.

10

"Showing Kindness to Our Neighbor"

St. Peter's Lutheran Church, Emden, IL

Kogudus Sunday, July 9, 1989

Welcome. I especially want to welcome those of you who've been at Kogudus this weekend and your families. It's great to have you here this morning. For our guests, Pastor Frank Pieper is our pastor, and he's on a busman's holiday. He's at a family gathering and is preaching there today. We wish him and Joyce a good vacation and a safe trip home.

Please pray with me as we begin. Jesus, we thank you for this morning that we may meet here together. Please bless this service that it may bring glory to you. In your name. Amen. The Gospel for today will be the text Luke 10:25-37. It's a great Gospel. There are some who say this Gospel, the story of the Good Samaritan, is one of the most superb classics on the subject of human kindness in all literature.

There was a Jewish lawyer who stood up to put Jesus to the test. He said, "*Teacher, what must I do to inherit eternal life?*" Jesus said to him, "*You're a lawyer. What is written in the law? How do you read it?*" And the lawyer answered, "*You shall love the Lord your God with all your heart and with all your soul and with all your strength and with all your mind—and your neighbor as yourself.*"

Jesus said to him, "*You have answered right. Do this and you will live.*"

But the lawyer, wishing to justify himself, said to Jesus, "*And who is my neighbor?*" At this point Jesus told a great story of kindness and compassion. The story of the Good Samaritan.

A man was going down the road from Jerusalem to Jericho and he fell among robbers who stole all he had, even stripping him of his clothes. They beat him and left him in the road half dead. Now, by chance, a Jewish priest was going down the road, and when he saw him, he passed by on the other side of the road. Likewise a Levite, a leader of the community, came along and when he saw the man, he too passed by on the other side. But a man from Samaria, a Samaritan, as he journeyed, he came to where the man was, and when he saw him, he had compassion and he went to him. He took oil and wine from his pack and he poured wine into his wounds and oil on them and he bound them up with bandages. Then he set him on his own animal and brought him to an inn.

The Living Bible says there he nursed him through the night. And the next day he took from his purse a day's wages and gave it to the innkeeper. "*Take care of him,*" he said. "*I'll soon be back this way and when I do I will stop and pay you whatever else you spend.*" "*Which of these three,*" said Jesus, "*do you think proved to be a neighbor to the man who fell among robbers?*" The lawyer replied, "*The one who showed mercy on him.*" And Jesus said to him, "*Go and do likewise.*" Jesus, no doubt, was the kindest man who ever lived. In the conclusion of the book of John, it says if all the kind things Jesus did were written down one by one, the whole world could not contain the books.

Jesus talked a great deal about kindness—just good old-fashioned kindness—like you and I are capable of doing. It seems as though Jesus would rather see kindness in us than any other trait. Of course, our kindness can't save us; Jesus saves us, but he sure seemed to like kindness and compassion. Jesus even said in Matthew 10 that not one single act of kindness toward our neighbor—no matter how small—would go unrewarded. Jesus put so much stress on this thing of kindness that he identifies himself with those who need it, and in effect, seems to tell us we cannot be friends with him and be indifferent to suffering.

Like the lawyer in today's Gospel we too try to define the word *neighbor*. We sometimes take great strides to try and locate him, but it seems like *neighbor* is not a generality to be defined, but an individual to be met. God, who governs even the fall of the sparrow, will define neighbor for us by laying him across the road—sometimes half dead—in front of us. No, we do not have to take great strides to find him, but like the priest and the Levite, we will have to take great strides if we are going to avoid him, and walk around on the other side of the road.

So who is our neighbor? Where is this person who needs our love and compassion? On July 4 Vicki and I decided to start celebrating early, so we went to Hardee's for breakfast. While we were there, a lady who we happen to know came over and talked with us. She said she was going to be seventy-seven in September. She went on to say that every morning her daughter picks her up and brings her to Hardee's for breakfast. She said instead of sitting home alone and drinking a cup of coffee, she gets up, gets dressed, and fixes her hair, looking forward to being with other people and getting out. Her eyes sparkled when she told us.

Some of us too often take steps to avoid our parents, and walk by on the other side where other things are happening. What about our kids?

Have we ever, like the priest or the Levite, looked at them and taken steps to pass by on the other side—the side of ridicule or put-down or forcing decisions on them, rather than to encourage and support them whenever possible? Other members of our family—our brothers and sisters? How many times has Jesus laid them in the road ahead of us, only for us to look—and pass by on the other side.

Some of you know my sister JoAnn. She and her husband, Tony, who many of you know, have always had a dream of building a new home in the hills outside of York, Pennsylvania, where Tony works for Caterpillar. A few years ago they bought an acreage up in the hills and planted several thousand Christmas trees, and this year—they did it! They built a new home and moved in this spring. Ten days ago, JoAnn went to the grocery store and came home without any groceries—and she didn't know why. She seemed exhausted and confused. They called the doctor and went to the hospital for tests. Last Wednesday they confirmed that JoAnn has multiple sclerosis.

Now JoAnn has someone to put oil on her wounds and bind them up. Tony is there with her and the doctors are there. Her children came from Florida, Maryland, and Tennessee to be with her over the Fourth of July—and four and a half grandchildren. But this week, as I read the Gospel over and over, getting ready for this morning, I thought a lot about JoAnn. Could it be that God has placed her in my path and I must take steps to either pass her by on the other side, or go to York where all I can possibly do is tell her I love her and I'm pulling for her and praying for remission?

What about those we work with or those we live by? What about those people who make us feel uncomfortable? Do we walk to them or do we take steps to avoid them and pass by on the other side? I know from my own life that the people who did not run away from my pain, but reached out to me with compassion, they brought new strength and healing to me!

Last night I heard John Cross give a really great talk at Camp Griesheim. At the beginning of his talk and again at the end, John challenged us with a couple of questions. One of those questions was "What is my ministry?" It's kind of a scary thing to talk about a ministry, especially for those of us who are lay people. But according to the Gospel for today, Jesus asks us only to meet our neighbor where he is and offer him kindness and compassion.

You know, when I think of it, that's not so hard, is it? Christ probably wants us right where we are, showing kindness to those around us—and you know what? No matter who or what he lays in the road ahead of us, he promises to give us the strength to do what he wants us to do.

We really don't even have to know very much. You see, people don't really care how much we know—if they know how much we care. Who then is my neighbor? Amen.

11

"Touched by God's Spirit"

St. Peter's Lutheran Church, Emden, IL

Pentecost—April 14, 1991

Five weeks from today will be Pentecost. It was on Pentecost over 1,950 years ago that God poured out his Holy Spirit upon his people and the church began.

God made his presence known to the apostles and a group of believers in a spectacular way. There was roaring wind and fire. People were able to proclaim God's message in different languages so everyone could understand the Gospel. It was a spectacular start for the church. From that time on, the church began to grow and spread out to what it is today.

On May 19 we will be celebrating Pentecost here at St. Peter's. At the worship committee meeting last week, we tried to think of a way to help make Pentecost extra special. It seemed as though what made that first Pentecost after Jesus' ascension so special was the fact that God's people were touched by his Spirit—so why not celebrate Pentecost this year by asking everyone who has been touched by God's Spirit to share something of that experience? So that's what is going to happen.

Everyone is invited to share a couple of sentences or a paragraph on your experience of being touched by God's Holy Spirit. Simply write it down, turn it in, or mail it to the church office by May 5. They will be compiled on an insert in the bulletin for Pentecost, May 19. Pastor may refer to them in his sermon.

"Whoa!" you say. "Hold on there! Nothing that spectacular ever happened to me." Don't be too sure. Think about it. Remember in the Old Testament the prophet Elijah needed a message from God. A mighty wind came along and Elijah looked for God in the wind, but God wasn't there. He then looked in an earthquake, but no God; and finally in a fire, but God's message wasn't there. God's message then came to Elijah in a still, small voice. God may use dramatic methods in your life, but for most of us, he comes in a still, small voice, usually a still, small voice of someone who cares for us.

I'm going to write down and turn in a couple of experiences that have been really special to me. Let me give you an example of one of them. Several years ago, Vicki, Todd, and I were driving home from Springfield hospital just after Tim died. For me it was the toughest day of my life. On the way home I thought—no one—I don't think even God himself can fully comprehend how I feel. We drove into the lane and went into the house. A car drove in right behind us. It was Ruth Reiners. Somehow she must have heard. I was wrong. There was someone who knew how I felt, because Ruth, too, had lost a son. Ruth came to the door, and in "a still, small voice" said, "You think you won't get through this, but I promise you that you will. I'll wash the dishes and clean the house. Your friends will be here soon." There was no doubt that God's Holy Spirit came to me in our kitchen that October day through Ruth Reiners.

So once more, think about it. When has someone reached out to you and helped you, or comforted you, or made you feel really good? Maybe someone older, maybe a child. Maybe in church, maybe somewhere else. Maybe when you thought no one cared for you, and a knock came at the door and a still, small voice said, "I made you some cookies," or "Do you want to talk awhile?"

God's Holy Spirit comes to us in many ways. That's what the church is, people caring for people around them. Write down your special time and turn it in and we will all celebrate Pentecost—the birth of the church—together on May 19.

12

"Sow a Few Mustard Seeds"

St. Peter's Lutheran Church, Emden, IL

Fathers' Day—June 16, 1991

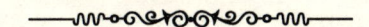

The text for today is taken from the Gospel according to Mark that Phyllis Struebing just read, the fourth chapter beginning with verse 26. Let's pray together before we start. Lord, thank you for this morning. Please bless our words and our thoughts that they may bring glory to you. Please be with all those involved with the Bible school the last two weeks, and bless their closing this morning during the second service. In your name we pray. Amen.

In the fourth chapter of Mark, Jesus has been teaching using parables. He has just explained the parable of the sower when the seeds fell on different kinds of soil, then the parable of the lamp under the bushel. He then went on to the message we are looking at today.

"The Kingdom is like this," Jesus said. "A man scatters seed in his field. He then sleeps at night, and he is up during the day—all the while the seeds *are silently sprouting and growing, and the man does not know how this happens—it just does. The soil itself makes the plants to grow, then bear fruit. First the tender stalk appears, then the head, and finally the head full of grain. Then when it is ripe harvest comes."*

Jesus goes on. He asks, "*What shall we say the kingdom of God is like? What parable shall we use to explain it? It's like this,*" he says, "*a man takes a mustard seed, one of the smallest of seeds, and plants it in the ground. After a while it grows up and becomes one of the biggest of plants. It puts out such large branches that the birds come and make nests in it.*"

Seeds sprouting and growing have been an unexplainable mystery, a miracle, since time began. The seed goes into the ground, and if conditions are right, sometimes in less than a week, it emerges.

For those of us who didn't get our planting done until the end of May or the first of June, where the ground was moist and the sun was hot, you could see down the bean rows in only five to six days. How does this happen? I guess these days, a plant breeder or an agronomist can tell us why it happens, but it's still pretty hard to explain exactly what happens. It's a miracle!

In the parable about the kingdom of God, Jesus seems to be talking about spiritual growth. We can better understand the process of spiritual growth by comparing it to the slow but certain growth of a plant. You can't see it happening, but it is.

Today is Fathers' Day—a day officially set aside, so I read in the *Courier* this week, by President Richard Nixon in 1972. Unofficially, Fathers' Day has been observed since June 19, 1910.

When I thought about the mustard seed, something very small and sort of insignificant, I thought about a child right after conception—also very small and sort of insignificant, but if everything goes okay, the child begins to grow and is soon born and grows up to become a man or woman—maybe even a parent.

Those of us who are parents, and especially today I can say to those of us who are fathers, what is one of the greatest things that we can do for our children? At an early age, begin to sow the seeds of the Gospel in their heart and mind so they can take root and begin to grow—spiritual growth! There are those who say we shouldn't do that—that's forcing Christianity on our children. But if we don't sow those seeds, how will they know? How can they make a decision whether or not to believe the Gospel if they don't know what it is or have never heard of it? The only way our children can have real freedom to choose is for them to know about Christ and what he has done for them. Then they can choose! The world will teach them the ways of the world. Who will acquaint them with Christ? At least today let's consider the job we fathers have.

At the second service this morning, the Bible school will be having their closing program. Some of the things taught here in Bible school the last two weeks will never be forgotten. Think for a moment—when you were between four and twelve or 13 years old. Can you remember anything significant you heard about Christ? I'll bet you can. At Bible school a seed is planted and it begins to grow. We fathers need to make sure that seed is planted in our children in Bible school, Sunday school, church, and at home.

I can still remember really well, before I was old enough to go to country school, getting ready to go to Sunday school at Union. Most of the time my dad was the only man in Sunday school. When I was getting this sermon ready, I got to thinking, "Wonder why Dad always went to Sunday school? Why hadn't I ever asked him?" So Friday evening I got in the truck and drove to his house. Many of you know my dad—he'll be eighty-two this summer.

I asked him, "Dad, why did you always go to Sunday school when all the other men waited and just came to church?"

"Well," he said, "I just thought it was the thing to do."

"Well," I asked, "did you and Mom ever talk about it?"

"No," he said, "I can't remember that we ever discussed it. We just went."

Now I'm not standing up here telling you my dad is better than your dad. Of course he isn't; and I'm not telling you he's better than you or me. I'm just telling you a story that meant a lot to me. Because, you see, by going to Sunday school, Dad sowed a seed in my life by showing me something that was important to him. And that seed has grown in me, and it's now very important for me to see that my kids and my grandchildren get to hear the Gospel. Does that make me better than someone else? Of course not. It simply helped me to understand about something that was very important.

And so for all of us fathers today, let's remember to sow a few of those mustard seeds. And then while we are sleeping at night, and while we are up during the day, all the while, those seeds will be silently sprouting and growing, even though we do not know how this happens—yet it does. Amen.

13

"The Gospel, St. Peter's, and Us"

St. Peter's Lutheran Church, Emden, IL

1997

Friday afternoon, Larry Zumwalt, our church council president, called and wanted to know if I could fill in this morning. He asked me because I had volunteered that if the council ran into a last minute emergency while we were in between pastors, I would be glad to do my best to help out. I had no idea it would be the first Sunday.

Please let us pray together. Jesus, please bless our service this morning. Help us to hear the Gospel and respond to it. In Jesus' name, Amen.

After Larry called, I came into the church to pick up a bulletin to see what the scripture readings for today were. I noticed that Pastor Larson's title for his sermon was "The Gospel, St. Peter's, and You." I thought, "That sounds pretty good." This is our first Sunday without Pastor Pieper. Where do we go from here?

I'm going to use Pastor Larson's theme, but change it slightly to "The Gospel, St. Peter's, and Us", because I'm really out there with you. For most of us lay people, I think the Gospel for today that I just read is kind of complex and confusing. Jesus was having trouble in his hometown of Nazareth. The people couldn't believe that Jesus was the Messiah—the Christ—the Savior. They knew him as the carpenter's son. They knew his father and mother, his brothers and his sisters. How could Jesus be the Son of God?

It seems as if their disbelief was so strong that Jesus didn't do very many miracles, and what miracles he did do didn't have much effect on the hometown crowd or change their ideas about him. So Jesus looked elsewhere, seeking out people who would respond to his message and his miracles. Later, as he went among the towns, he called his disciples to him and sent them out to proclaim his message, and he gave them power to do miracles. He said, *"Take nothing with you; no money, no bread, only one coat, your staff, and wear your sandals. Preach to those who will listen, and to those won't, shake the dust off your feet and go on, leave town."*

Don't you think this is kind of confusing? Why didn't Jesus just keep preaching and doing miracles until they couldn't help but believe? Why didn't he tell his disciples, "If the people won't listen, then you stay right there until they do"? Let's take another look at this. What is the message here that Jesus has for us in today's Gospel, "The Gospel, St. Peter's, and Us?" Could it be that the listeners of the Gospel are responsible for what they do with the message after they hear it? And could it be that we are not responsible when others reject Christ's message of salvation, but that we do have the responsibility to share it as best we can? I think this is what the "Gospel" in "The Gospel, St. Peter's, and Us," is about today—our responsibility to listen and to tell others.

What does this mean to St. Peter's? That might be the easy part. As a congregation, we are to proclaim the Gospel to everyone faithfully and responsibly.

Okay, the Gospel, we've talked about, and St. Peter's, we've talked about. What about us? That's where it becomes hard. This is where the rubber hits the road. How can we, personally and individually, tell others about the message of Christ?

This is too hard. Sure, it's easy for me this morning. Like I heard a guy say the other day, "This is what they pay me the big money for." Seriously, it is easier because you expect to hear it from the pulpit. But it is hard in the streets, or in our businesses, farms or school, or work, or in our homes with our family. Let's think about that for a moment. Maybe it's not quite as hard as it seems. Could it be that we are doing some of that now and not realizing it? Are we doing something, anything, to make a difference? "But what can I do?" we ask.

"The Gospel, St. Peter's, and Us." What can we do? We can love and care for the people God has placed around us. And we can help keep the Gospel alive because the Gospel can still change lives. Maybe it won't change all lives, but it will change lives. We can influence people even if we think we can't. Whatever we do has a ripple effect. It goes on and on.

This is Fourth of July weekend. Two hundred and twenty-one years ago, our country signed our Declaration of Independence. Since Vicki and I went to Estonia and Russia, I have a different outlook and appreciation for freedom. I'm free, you're free, our families are free because some of you and your families' ancestors sacrificed time, money, and their very lives so that you and I can still celebrate Independence Day. I did nothing to deserve it, but because of the ripple effect that came from other's love and sacrifice, my family and I and all of us enjoy freedom today. What we do can influence people, sometimes for a long, long time. Jesus and his disciples changed the world, and we can make a difference.

I read a story about a woman who influenced the people who God placed around her. The story is one of many from a book called *"Chicken Soup for the Soul,"* and is about a Catholic sister who was a teacher in Minnesota. We all have an opportunity to influence the people around us—either in a good way or in a not-so-good way. But what makes the difference, the real difference in how we love and care for those around us? It's knowing that we do it for Christ. He makes the difference.

"The Gospel, St. Peter's, and Us." For those of you who were here last Sunday, you heard Pastor Pieper tell the story of a pastor who was about to retire. He said when he was a young man, he felt his congregation was like people in an over-turned boat in the middle of the river, and he was standing on the shore shouting instructions, trying to save them. Then as a middle-aged pastor, he envisioned his congregation as people in an over-turned boat, and he was now down off the shore and in the water, still shouting instructions to save them. Now the pastor said, "As I near retirement, I feel I'm in the middle of the river with the people and we're all trying to encourage and save each other." I later told Pastor that I never felt that he was ever anywhere but in the water with us, always encouraging us, always supporting us as we encouraged others, and allowing us to support and encourage him.

"The Gospel, St. Peter's, and Us." Yes, we are all in the water, but together we can keep the message of the Gospel alive. Amen.

14

"Move Our Fence?"

Delavan Presbyterian Church

January 9, 2005

Good morning. My wife, Vicki, and I want to thank you for asking us here today. It's a little like coming home. I started my life as a Presbyterian, being born and baptized in the Presbyterian Church at Union about seven miles east of Emden. One of my first paid jobs during my grade school years was working at the church as the janitor. I cleaned the church and built a fire in the coal furnace during cold weather. I got one dollar per week. During the winter my dad would let me drive the International M tractor to the church on Saturday night or early Sunday morning to build the fire so the church would be warm when everyone arrived.

When Vicki and I were married, the church was about to close, so I joined Vicki's church, St. Peter's Lutheran in Emden, where we are still members today. So even though I am now Lutheran, I still remember those days at the Union Presbyterian Church. A lot of Sundays my dad was the only man in Sunday school and I suppose it was because of him that I developed the habit of going to Sunday school.

Vicki and I farmed and lived in the Hartsburg-Emden area all our lives. We still farm there, but years ago we bought a home north of town out on Delavan Road. It was a big move for us. Neither of us had ever had an address other than in Hartsburg-Emden and we didn't know about moving so far away from home.

Jim Haycock asked if I would be interested in speaking here this morning, and if I was involved in prison ministry. I said yes, I would like to come and be with you, and yes, I'm still somewhat involved, but I no longer go into prisons myself. There are some men in the eastern part of the state who are still able to go in for weekend retreats that I keep in touch with.

Some of us from this area first started going into prisons in 1974 when we were invited to Montana State Prison by the chaplain there. After that, we went to Menard Prison at Chester, Illinois. We also went to Danville, Taylorville, Robinson, Centralia, and two prisons in Wisconsin.

There's just a couple of things I would like to share with you about prisons in Illinois. When we started going in, there were less than eight thousand adults incarcerated in the state. There are now forty-three thousand adults locked up in state correctional centers. This doesn't include jails and federal prisons.

In 1970 there were eleven adult facilities in the state and today there are forty-two. The Illinois Department of Corrections' budget for 2003 was $1,206,607,900. That figures out to an average of $20,929 per adult inmate per year, approximately the same cost per year as a really good university.

So what's my point? Isn't there some way that at least some of the people can be cared for and educated enough or loved enough that this trend could be reversed? Please keep this thought in mind as we continue.

Let's pray a moment. Thank you, Father, for this morning, for this church, and for those who worship here. Please let what is said here bring glory to you. In Jesus' name. Amen.

The Gospel today, I believe, has a great message. Now I'm not a theologian, so you don't have to agree with all or any of my thoughts. If it makes sense to you—fine. If it doesn't, think about it for a while, then throw it away, but come back next Sunday because next Sunday's speaker will probably be a lot better.

I want to read this story again. I'm going to read it from a new translation called *The Message*, and I want to back up to the beginning of the chapter so we can see what is taking place here. Please listen with me. (Matthew 3 from *The Message*)

We have just experienced Christmas, a time of miracles. We now have fast-forwarded to Jesus' baptism, the beginning of his ministry. I know that Christmas is for me and you—for everyone. But, Jesus' baptism—what was that for? John said that Jesus' baptism—in other words, the people that Jesus would baptize—would be much better than his. But Jesus came to John and asked John to baptize him. Why did Jesus ask to be baptized? It was not for repentance of his sins. Jesus never sinned.

After studying this, I believe there are several reasons. Jesus was showing support for what John was doing. Jesus was starting his public ministry. He was identifying himself with the others who were baptized. He wanted to be obedient to God—and God did show his approval. "*This is my beloved Son in whom I am well pleased.*" But, I believe there is one more reason that stands out. Through Jesus' baptism he was asking for forgiveness not for himself, but confessing sin on behalf of us all. I believe that was the first sign other than prophecy that Jesus was going to take our sin and die for us. At that point, God's grace came alive for us through Jesus. He took our sins and dealt with them in a way that was impossible for us. That's *grace*. We don't deserve it, but he did it anyway.

I wonder if this was the first time it became really real to Jesus. I don't know if he knew all this from his youth or not, but remember right after his baptism, he went out into the wilderness and fasted for forty days. Some people think this became so real to Jesus, this taking the sin of the world on himself, that he went and thought about it so deeply, he couldn't eat for forty days. It literally took his appetite away. I don't know. It's something to think about. Yes, this was the beginning—Jesus getting ready to die for you and me—for the whole world.

We've been baptized, too. What does this mean for us? How do we treat our neighbors—the rest of the world? Those we don't like very well or those who think differently, or have been raised differently than we have? What about those people in prison we talked about earlier? What about those who don't go to church, or those who don't treat us like we think they should?

Let me tell you a story in closing. During World War I there were four men who had been together for a long time, fighting side by side across the countryside. They were fortunate that none of them had been seriously injured. But then on one particular day when the battle was ferocious, one of them was mortally injured. The remaining three were devastated. They carried their friend to a grove of trees and covered him with leaves until they could come back for him. That night they came back to the grove with a stretcher and they carried him a couple of miles to a church they had remembered passing several days earlier. There was a cemetery by the church and they wanted to bury their friend there. When they got to the church, they went inside. To their surprise, a priest was there praying. They explained their plight to the priest and asked if they could bury their fellow comrade in the cemetery. "Of course," the priest said, and he showed them where to bury their friend. As they started to dig, the priest said to them, "Your friend, he is Catholic, isn't he?"

"Why, no he isn't," they said. "Well this is a Catholic Cemetery. I'm afraid you can't bury him here, but you can bury him over there, right outside the fence."

They were hurt, but a war was going on and they had to get back so they buried their friend outside the fence. When they finished they made a vow that they would come back in the morning and put up a simple marker.

Early the next morning, before sunup, the men arrived at the cemetery. They looked and looked, but they couldn't find the grave. They walked up and down the fence, thinking maybe the grave had been covered up with leaves because the wind had blown hard all night, but they couldn't find it. Suddenly the priest came out of the church and joined the men.

"We can't find our friend's grave," they said. "We've looked and looked. You saw us bury him last night. What has happened?"

The priest said, "Come, I'll show you. Here he is inside the fence. Last night I couldn't sleep. I rolled and tossed until after midnight. I kept thinking about telling you that you couldn't bury your friend in our cemetery. I was wrong. I knew I was wrong. Finally I got up wondering what I could do. How could I make this right? And then I knew. I worked all night. I moved the fence. Your friend is now included in our cemetery. May God bless his soul and ours."

Is this what we need to do? Move our fence? We want people to be like us and then we will accept them. But people are different. People are unique. If we would move our fences over, maybe some of those young people we talked about earlier wouldn't end up in prison. Maybe if we moved our fence, other people would feel loved and accepted in our church. Jesus moved his fence when he went down into the waters and said, "John, baptize me—do it. My people need forgiveness and I'm the only one who can do it." Jesus kept moving his fence, clear to the cross. Even while dying, he prayed for those who put him to death, *"Forgive them, Father."*

May God bless us all as we lean on our fences and think about Jesus' baptism and our baptism, and God's wonderful grace. Amen.

15

"Blessed by God"

St. John's Lutheran Church, Hartsburg, IL

January 20, 2005

Prayer: Help us, Father, to listen to the Gospel today and to be thankful for where you have placed us. Please bless this church and those who worship here, and their families. In your name. Amen.

The Gospel for the day is the text for this presentation, Matthew 5:1-12. The words of the beatitudes seem to contradict each other, but God's way of living usually contradicts the world—or another way to say it is that God's way usually contradicts our way. If you decide you want to live for God, it seems as though you must be willing to give when others take, to love when others hate, to help when others abuse. I believe what Jesus is saying here is by giving up your own rights to help and serve others, you will one day receive everything God has in store for you.

Is that right? Can that be true? Can you do that? Can I do that? Probably not, but isn't that what we want God to do? When others take from us, we say, "Please, God, give me something." When others seem to hate us, we say, "Please, Jesus, love me." When people are abusing us, we say, "Please, God, send your Holy Spirit to help me." It's the way we want God to treat us, but we don't always do very well in the way we treat others.

When God does that—that's what grace is. When he blesses us when we don't deserve it, that's what grace is. I don't know if you remember—about three weeks ago, the Gospel for the day was Matthew 3:13-17. John was baptizing people in the Jordan River and Jesus came there and wanted John to baptize him. John was reluctant. He said, "*I am not worthy.*" He wanted Jesus to baptize him, but Jesus said, "*Do it, John, do it.*" Why did Jesus want to be baptized? It was not for the forgiveness of his sins. Jesus never sinned. It was for the world's sin—for you and for me. That was grace. Jesus did for us what we didn't deserve, but now Jesus tells us, if you like that forgiveness—if you appreciate that grace—then this is how you should live.

The beatitudes are the heart of Jesus' teaching, and some people say the Sermon on the Mount, or the beatitudes, is to the New Testament what the Ten Commandments are to the Old Testament. Each beatitude tells how to be blessed by God. Blessed means more than happiness. It implies the fortunate state of those who are in God's kingdom. The beatitudes don't promise laughter or pleasure or earthly prosperity. Being blessed by God means to experience the hope and joy of heaven. It's understanding God's grace.

So what does that have to do with the Israeli Jews and the Palestinians? Let me share with you some things that Vicki and I saw in the Holy Land. (Shows pictures from the Holy Land.)

The following story was submitted by The Reverend Ann Leesman-Helmke, Gandhi Peace Delegation U.S. Coordinator:

August 2004, and in the land where Christianity was born, Jerry and Vicki traveled as part of the Gandhi Peace Delegation to the Holy Land. Arun Gandhi, Mahatma Gandhi's grandson, led the delegation, along with official representatives from the Lutheran, Presbyterian, and Roman Catholic Churches. The delegates met with key leaders as well as the common folk of the land.

While staying in Jerusalem, some of their delegation's stops included:

- meeting with farmers in Qalquilya, Tulkarem, and Jayyous,
- assessing medical care with Bishop Munib Younan from the Evangelical Lutheran Church in Jordan and the Holy Land at the Lutheran World Federation's Augusta Victoria Hospital on the Mt. Of Olives,
- attending peace rallies in Abu Dis (where Mary, Martha, and Lazarus lived) and Ramallah,
- touring the Old City of Jerusalem and meeting Jewish, Christian, and Muslim faith leaders,
- meeting officially with Yasser Arafat and the Palestinian Prime Minister (the Gandhi Delegation was the last official delegation to meet with Arafat before his death),
- meeting officially with members of the Israeli Knesset and authors of the peace plan, the Geneva Accord, and
- participating with a crowd of thousands at a candlelight prayer vigil in Bethlehem's Manger Square.

For those who knew Jerry and are reading this, it will come as no surprise that he touched everyone deeply in the Holy Land, but he especially touched the simple Palestinian farmers as he wept compassionate tears for their great losses of land and crop. Jerry understood that "God's way of living usually contradicts the world . . . usually contradicts our way." One might have observed Arun Gandhi as the leader of the delegation, but for those of us who traveled together that hot August, we came to know that Jerry was the deep spiritual leader of our group.

16

"Born Again"

St. Peter's Lutheran Church, Emden, IL

Laity Sunday—April 10, 2005

The second reading for this third Sunday of Easter—Laity Sunday—is taken from I Peter 1:17-23. I'd like to focus on verse 23 for just a few moments and I would like to first read it from the New Living translation. It seems easier for me to understand. Verse 23: *"For you have been born again. Your new life didn't come from your earthly parents because the life they gave you will end in death. But this new life will last forever because it comes from the eternal living Word of God."*

Born again—a much-quoted phrase in Christian circles. Jesus himself used it. He said you must be born again. In John 3:3, Jesus said, *"I assure you unless you are born again—you cannot see the Kingdom of God."* How can we know if we are born again?

Sometimes I feel the Christian life is not that complicated. Simply believe and you will be saved. John 3:16 says, *"For God so loved the world that He gave His only Son that whosoever believeth in Him shall not perish, but have eternal life."* That's simple enough. But then today in verse 23 Peter says you have been born anew or you have been born again. Have I? Have you? It almost seems like we need a little proof here. I want to tell you a story.

There were two farmers. They had always gotten along well. They saw each other fairly often. They went to the same church. They even went to a retreat together once. But then, as things sometimes happen, one of them did something that really hurt the other one, and one day on the main street of their hometown, they met and anger rang out. Later when they would meet, even though they didn't argue, things were not the same. This went on for a couple of years. Then during Lent, a couple of weeks before Easter, the two farmers met at church. One of them approached the other from behind and put his arm around the other and held him very close; in fact, tight against him. They looked each other in the eye and the one who was doing the holding said, "A couple of weeks ago, I went to a funeral, and there I was able to see that life is short. You and I are not right with each other. I got really mad at you once and I can't go on with this between us." He paused a moment and then said, "I'm asking you to forgive me. I want you to please forgive me."

The second farmer said, "Well, I'm sorry I hurt you."

But the first farmer said, "I don't care about that. I don't care what happened at the start, I just want you to please forgive me." How could a grown man make such an apology? How could he be brave enough—have enough courage—to risk himself in such a way? I believe there is only one way. Somewhere down through the years this man was born again. Was it at his baptism or at confirmation when he renewed his baptismal vows? Was it one evening when he said his daily prayers?

Was it at the funeral? I don't know when it was, but how else could he have reached this capacity? To me this man was a man among men, a man who sometime in his life was born again.

I know this story because I was the second farmer. Not the courageous one—not the one who reached out. I was simply the one who saw a man, who I believe, sometime in his life, was born again. How did this make me feel? The meaning of Easter was pretty real to me, and hopefully, this will help give me the courage to act like I've been born again.

This is Laity Sunday. Peter said you have been born anew. May God give us all the courage to live that out. Amen.

Part II

Organizational Meetings

17. "Opportunities for Christ"—Luther League Rally, October 14, 1973 93
18. "God Has Work for You to Do"—Lutheran Brotherhood Convention, November 3, 1974 101
19. "Who Are We?"—Lutheran Brotherhood Supper, January, 1984 113
20. "Tell Your Children What You Believe"—Woodstock Prayer Breakfast, May 2, 1987 121
21. "Two Treasures"—St. Peter's LYO Supper & Program—2002 129

17

"Opportunities for Christ"

Luther League Rally

October 14, 1973

A song is not a song until you sing it.
A bell is not a bell until you ring it.
Love wasn't put into your heart to stay—
Love—it isn't even love until you give it away.

Our faith and our love go together. Our faith is no good unless we give it away. We have to tell others about Jesus Christ, but this isn't easy for us. In our society, talking about Jesus just isn't done very much. Why? Is it because we don't see any reason to? Is it because we don't have time? Or is it because down deep, we really don't believe it?

I think that as Christians, we sometimes need to go back—way back—and give some really serious thought about our Christian lives. I think that every once in a while, we should stop and renew our faith, and see if we feel all of this Jesus talk is true, or just a bunch of nonsense.

That's what I would like to do with you today. Go back and search out some answers to questions that we have, like, is the Bible just a fantasy or is it truth? Did some supreme being create this earth or did it just happen? Who was this man that Christians call Jesus? Did he really die so that I might never die? Will he come back, or are we just kidding ourselves?

Let's start at the beginning. Let's start with the Christian textbook, the Bible. The Bible is a book that was written by men, but inspired by God. If this is true . . . or wait . . . who says it is true? I don't believe anyone can prove it. I mean iron-clad proof like two and two is four, or . . . or what? What can we really prove?

Here is where a word called faith enters in. We have faith that the sun will come up every morning, faith it will go down at night. Faith that when we get hungry, we will find food to nourish our bodies, and faith that when we are tired, we can lie down and somehow, through some mysterious action, we go to sleep and later wake up refreshed, hopefully, and ready to start a new day.

The Bible tells us that God created all things. If the Bible isn't truth, we are living in a world of coincidence. If God didn't make the earth and all its splendor, we sure are lucky that things turned out so exact. Let me give you an example. The earth now rotates on its axis once every twenty-four hours at the rate of one thousand miles per hour. What if it rotated instead at the rate of one hundred miles per hour? If it did, the earth's days and nights would then be ten times longer than they are now, with the end result being that the sun would burn all vegetation, and whatever was left, the long cold nights would freeze. If this is a coincidence, we sure are lucky.

The moon is 240,000 miles away from the earth. If the moon was only fifty thousand miles away, the tides of the ocean would be so huge that all the mountains on various continents would soon be eroded, and we would have storms and hurricanes every day. We sure are lucky that such a coincidence took place.

Suppose we were walking along and looked down on the ground and found a watch, but we didn't know what it was because we had never seen one before. And suppose we studied it and found that when we wound the stem, it would, in turn, tighten a spring inside and cause the watch to run. And after two revolutions of the small hand, we would discover a day had passed. Suppose we studied all the small gears and springs inside, and the jewels that helped to balance the motion of the instrument, and we noticed the glass crystal on the front that seals out the dirt, and the stainless steel back that doesn't rust, and the numbers on the dial, and the words "waterproof" and "shockproof," and seventeen jewels on the back. Would we then come to the conclusion that all of these pieces, after turning and rolling for millions of years, had been formed and in some freak act of nature, they were all hurled or slid together so they became a precision instrument?

How foolish! If we wanted to study a watch, and wanted to know about it, we would look almost immediately for the watchmaker. If we want to study the earth and the galaxies that have turned and rotated with precision for these thousands of years, bringing forth times and seasons, rain and sunshine, doesn't it make sense to look immediately for the earth maker?

My point is this: I have faith that the Bible is truth. I can see no other way.

Okay, let's suppose you buy the fact that God did make the earth and all its splendor—that the first part of the Bible is true. When the Bible ends the story of creation, it almost immediately begins the prophecies and the promises of the coming of the Promised One, the Prince of Peace, the Messiah. And with the birth of Jesus, they all start coming true, thousands of years later, and the prophecies in the Old Testament as to how the people would turn on him and eventually hang him on a cross.

Who was this man called Jesus? Here again we have to make a decision. Many claim he never existed. They say the Bible is wrong in declaring the birth of such a person. Some say he was a great man, maybe even a prophet. These people believe he lived here, did a few miracles or tricks, preached the word, and probably went one step too far and died, probably by crucifixion. But Christians say much more. They say he was the Promised One, the Prince of Peace, the Son of God, and that he still lives.

Now you may say, "I don't want to make a decision about this man. I don't want to offend anyone so I will stay neutral." By doing this, you have made your decision. We either accept Christ or we reject him. There is no middle ground. We are either for him or against him. Everyone who hears about him makes a decision. There is no way out.

If I told you that I was the Son of God, you would then have to decide if I was God's Son or if I was a liar. To those who say Jesus was merely a great man, or even a prophet, I say the same thing. He said he was the Son of God. Either he was or he was a liar. Again, there is no in between with Jesus.

Let's go ahead and assume for the time being that the Bible is true pertaining to Jesus being God's Son. Where do we fit in? The Bible was written, beginning with Genesis, thousands of years ago. Can this possibly be relevant to us? Is there any way we can fit into these writings? I tell you we *are* in those writings. We *are* a part of the Bible.

At the end of the Old Testament (the Book of the prophet Malachi) and the beginning of the New Testament (the Book of Matthew), there lies a span of silence—four hundred years. From the time Malachi cried in chapter four, verse two, *"the Sun of Righteousness will rise with healing in His wings,"* talking about the coming of Jesus, to the time of John the Baptist shouting in the wilderness in Matthew 3:3, *"Prepare a road for the Lord,"* no biblical prophet spoke or wrote. That was the beginning of the end of the waiting for the first coming of Jesus Christ.

After the last book of the New Testament, Revelation, was written, 1,900 and some odd years have passed, and again, a period of silence. We are in this period and it is the period of the second coming of Jesus Christ. In Revelation it tells of the tremendous events on earth and in heaven just before, during, and after his coming, and no matter how much time may intervene between Revelation and Christ's second coming, we can be sure—sure that the next thing on the program is this very thing—*Christ is coming again!*

Okay! Wow! Now what do we do? Where do we go from here? *Read God's Word.* That's where the action is. That's where it's all at. Get yourself a Living Bible or The Way, it's easier reading, and read! *Pray diligently and constantly.* I don't mean you have to be on your knees all day, but be always conscious of God's power and God's grace.

Listen for God! God is speaking to you in many ways: through the Bible, through other people, through your lives and your mind and your conscience. We must listen for God and to God.

Go to church. Many of us don't like to go to church. Many of us say our church doesn't have what we want or need. Then there are some who even say, "Our church is dead." We are the church. The church isn't a building. It's God's people reading, learning, sharing, loving, and waiting for Jesus' second coming.

Last Sunday several of us from our church had the opportunity to attend a Living Witness Institute in Minonk at the Emmanuel Lutheran Church there. After an afternoon of training, we went in teams of three (one leader and two prayer partners) and went to people's homes to share our faith with those living in that community.

The first question we asked the people was, "If you were to die tonight and stand before God, and he was to ask you, 'Why should I let you into my heaven?' What would your answer be?"

What would your answer be? Would God let you into his heaven? Why should he? Everyone falls short of the glory of God. Everyone breaks the Ten Commandments. No one can get to heaven by only good works and deeds, because we all fall short of God's laws and his glory.

Jesus came and died for us. He took our place. God has judged every person guilty and condemned him to death. Someone must pay for these sins and wrongdoings we have brought against God . . . but God loves us. He loves us so much that he couldn't stand to see us condemned. So he came through his son—and died for us.

When I look at the cross, I don't see just Jesus on the cross. I see myself hanging there, because I should be there. I made the sins, I should pay for them. But God said, "No! Let me do it. Let me take your place." He died, not just for a group of people, but for each one of us individually.

If Jesus would have written down a list of names of all the people he was dying for, our names would have been on that list. If you were the only person on earth, he would still have died for you because he loves you so much.

Give some 100% time to the Lord. This may be a weekend retreat or it may be alone in your room. But do something where you can devote a set amount of time to Christ with no interference. See how close you will come to him. See how you can feel the Holy Spirit if we only give ourselves to him. I mean get things cleared between you and your Lord. Get the feeling of assurance of eternal life. There is joy in this, and there is great comfort.

Tell others about Jesus. I was told last Sunday at the Living Witness Institute that ninety-eight percent of the people have never said anything to anyone about Jesus Christ. Only two percent of the people are actually sharing their faith with others. A man who visited our country, after two weeks, made the statement, "I thought the United States was a Christian nation. I sure was wrong. I never hear anyone talk about Jesus Christ."

Could this mean that although many of us call ourselves Christians, that only two percent know *for sure* that Christ died for us so that we may live forever? We must tell them. Jesus wants us to. He says there is much rejoicing over one sinner that repents. There will also be much joy and much reward for the person who lets the Holy Spirit work through him to help bring this person to Christ.

I Peter 2:10 says, *"Once you were less than nothing, but now you are God's very own. Once you knew little of God's kindness, but now your very lives have been changed by it."*

Have your lives been changed by Christ? Have you let Jesus into your heart? You may have gone to church all your life, but have never let God change your life and take control. Talk to your pastor, he will help you. Listen for God, he will instruct you. Don't listen just with your ears, but with your mind and your heart!

Hopefully and prayerfully, we can say as the apostle Paul said in his letter to the Philippians in 1:21, *"For me to live is opportunities for Christ."* Amen. My prayers go with you all.

18

"God Has Work for You to Do"

Lutheran Brotherhood Convention,

Peoria, Illinois

November 3, 1974

I would like to begin by reading 1 Timothy 6:20: "*Oh, Timothy, don't fail to do these things that God has entrusted to you.*"

In Paul's first letter to Timothy, he begins by saying, "*From: Paul, a missionary of Jesus Christ, sent out by the direct command of God our Savior and by Jesus Christ our Lord—our only hope. To: Timothy. Timothy, you are like a son to me in the things of the Lord. May God our Father and Jesus Christ our Lord show you his kindness and mercy and give you great peace of heart and mind*" (1:1-2 LB).

Paul loved Timothy. He loved him with all his heart. He loved him as a father loves a son. Just as God wants the best for us, Paul wanted the best for

Timothy. He wanted him to have all and be all that God intended him to be, and out of Paul's love for Timothy came this pleading statement: *"Timothy, don't fail (don't fail!) to do these things that God has entrusted to you"* (1:20a).

Yes, Paul, the greatest of all missionaries loved Timothy. And in his second letter to Timothy, chapter 1:13-14, he says, *"Hold tightly to the pattern of truth I taught you, especially concerning the faith and love Christ Jesus offers you. Guard well the splendid, God-given ability you received as a gift from the Holy Spirit who lives within you."*

Is God speaking to us here? Can we read Paul's letters to Timothy and say God is speaking to *us*? Has God given to us a pattern of truth concerning the faith and love of Jesus Christ, and do we, as verse 14 says, have a God-given ability that we received as a gift from the Holy Spirit who lives within us? Yes, we *do* and we *can*. We do have a God-given ability and we can be sure God is speaking to us through his words that he spoke through Paul to Timothy.

That's what I want to talk about this evening. That's what I want to share with you. First of all, the pattern of truth—the greatest of all truths, the *Gospel of Jesus Christ*. And secondly, what are we, *the men of the church,* going to do about it?

If we have a God-given ability we have received as a gift from the Holy Spirit, can we just ignore that? There's only one Holy Spirit—the same Holy Spirit that Jesus was talking about when he said, *"I must go now so the Comforter may come."* The same Holy Spirit that came to the apostles. The same Holy Spirit that is a part of our *tremendous* and *Holy* Triune God. Now if God has given us a gift, again—what are we going to do about it?

Let there be no doubt in our minds about our gifts, or our abilities. So many times when we think of gifts or abilities given to us by God, we think of people like the apostles, or Billy Graham, or our pastor, and we feel that either we don't have an ability, or if we do, it's so insignificant God won't notice, or care, or even expect us to use it.

Don't—please don't underestimate God's love for you. God has a job for you—not in general—but specific. God has a specific job for you to do, and if you don't do it, who will? There isn't any way I know of that I can stand up here and stress enough the fact that God loves you so much that he wants to include you in his work. In the only thing that really matters on this wonderful yet sometimes mixed-up earth, God says to you, "I want you to help me, please help me with my work." Or he may be saying, "I need to go over here and work. Come with me."

What do we say to this? Can we say, "Father, I can't, I'm too busy—or I'm not able, I'm not qualified." Maybe our problem is that we just can't trust him that much. You know, if we can't trust him that much, it's because we don't know him well enough. After Paul knew him really well, he trusted him completely in *all* things. Maybe we can't believe he's that real, that understanding, that loving—so full of warmth and grace—that *personal* to each one of us.

What does Jesus mean to us? I mean, really mean to us? Jesus means life—real life forever. That's great, nothing can beat that; but what about now? What does he mean to you and me now, besides living forever?

Deuteronomy 31:8 (RSV) says, *"It is the Lord who goes before you; he will be with you, he will not fail you or forsake you; do not fear or be dismayed."*

Psalm 32:8 (LB) says, *"I will instruct you, says the Lord, and guide you along the best pathway for your life; I will advise you and watch your progress."* That is personal. God promises to be by our side, not just when things are going good, or when we are in trouble, but all the time.

God promises not only to be with us if we accept Jesus, he promises to be in us. Okay, if God promises us all this, and we know God never backs down on a promise—he never has yet—if he promises all this, then why, why aren't our lives the kind of lives we want them to be? Why aren't we the obedient-and-obey-type Christian we all want to be?

I think this is the biggest question in my life right now. Why aren't I what I want to be, but more importantly, what God wants me to be? He has done *everything* for me. What's wrong? Has this thought ever been in your mind? What's wrong with me? Or do you think you're all God wants you to be?

Revelation 3:17 (LB) says, *"You say, 'I'm rich, with everything I want; I don't need a thing!'"* It then goes on to say, *"You don't realize that spiritually you are wretched and miserable and poor and blind, and naked."* Now I realize God is directing this letter to the church at Laodicea, but are any of us all God wants us to be? Can any of us say, "I am living my life completely for God and letting him guide my every footstep"? I don't think any of us can make such a statement. But I do believe that we as Christians can say that, at certain special times in our lives, maybe at communion or at a child's baptism, or when we first realized and accepted Jesus as our Savior, we have come close for that short period of time to being what God wants us to be, only to fall back.

I really believe that we as Christians should read Revelation 2 every day. In the letter to the church at Ephesus, John's pen, under the direction of God, is telling the people, *"I know how many good things you are doing. I have watched your hard work and your patience. You have patiently suffered for me without quitting."* But then in verse 4, God speaks to us directly, pouring out his feelings to us. He says, *"Yet there is one thing wrong: you don't love me as at first!"* Think about those times when you first loved Jesus—or those high times we were talking about a moment ago—at communion, or a child's baptism. Jesus says to us, *"You don't love me like you did then."*

What does Jesus mean? I think he is saying there are many good and beautiful things going on in the church right now. This pleases the Lord and glorifies him and that is great. But all these fine qualities in and for the church do not fully satisfy Jesus. It is a warm, loving, personal relationship with himself that he seeks. Jesus is even more interested in our relationship with him than what we do for him.

We need to be careful, lest we become so busy with things of the kingdom, that we do not have time for the best—abiding in the love of Christ. Love Jesus as he wants and deserves and the things of the kingdom, all the works and good deeds, will be naturally taken care of. Love Jesus for who he is—our Savior, yet even more than our Savior, *our Lord*. But to do this takes more than just being the Christian that most of us are. It takes commitment—total commitment to Jesus. And that total commitment takes the total giving of oneself, the total process of humbling oneself. We have to go down before we can go up. We have to go down on our knees before we can really go up to Jesus.

In the book *"Wayfarer in the Land"* by Hannah Hurnard, she writes about a stream of water "singing over and over again the song of all running water, that the lower one goes, the happier and fuller life becomes."

It's hard to humble oneself. When we as men, for instance, run our families, take care of our business, or perform our responsibilities in someone else's business, when people look to us for decisions all day long, it's hard to get into a frame of mind so we can humble ourselves. Did you ever see anyone wearing a big button that says, "When you are as great as I am, it's hard to be humble"? Well, this is kind of funny, yet in our minds, we may be really thinking this. To humble ourselves daily takes, for most of us, a renewal, a daily renewal, a putting aside of ourselves, and turning ourselves over to Jesus Christ and the things he has instructed us to do, to depend solely and entirely on him.

This spring I heard a tape from the district convention here in Peoria. Many of you, no doubt, were there. On the tape a pastor stated that every morning when he woke up, he said, "Good morning, Lord, I love you. What have you got for me to do today?" Can we say that? Can we turn our busy lives over to Jesus and put him first? This is daily renewal. Again, this is hard to do, and I think as Christians, yes, even as Christians, we need a renewal in our lives before we can experience this daily renewal.

I have become involved, as have a lot of other people across the United States, in one type of renewal experience. It's called Kogudus. Kogudus is an Estonian word meaning "Christian fellowship." I would like to share just a few things with you about Kogudus, but first I want to make it clear, just as clear as I possibly can, that Kogudus is just one of the many ways, just one of the many tools, that the Lord makes available to us. Kogudus is simply a weekend retreat, and just because you may decide to go doesn't mean you have a special seat in heaven. It isn't the end of your spiritual training, it's just one way that can be used along the way. I want to emphasize very strongly that if a person goes to a Kogudus and would by the grace of God come home a more humble, loving Christian, it is in no way because of Kogudus, but because of *Christ*.

Kogudus, as I said before, is an Estonian word for Christian fellowship, a weekend retreat that starts on Friday evening and ends on Sunday afternoon. It simply is a presentation on the Apostles' Creed, what it says, and what it means to all of us, combined with the Gospel, the importance of the sacraments, with special emphasis on what Jesus did and is doing for us. We also seem to become more aware of the love and concern we need for the people around us. This is put together with a special thrust to help us be aware of the need to go back to our church and go to work; we as laymen have a job, and that job is a part of the Great Commission, going back to our church, not because we have to, but because we want to.

Our church, that's where it's at. That's where the real action is, serving the Lord through our church. You see, if it wasn't for the church, the organized church—what would we have? Where would we be? It's the church that, through the years, has kept the sacraments, but more importantly, I think than anything, has kept alive the Word of God—the Word itself—Jesus

Christ. The Word that tells us in 1 Peter 2: 9 and 10 (RSV): *"God called you out of the darkness into His wonderful light. Once you were less than nothing; now you are God's own. Once you knew very little of God's kindness; now your very lives have been changed by it."* I love my church. I love the church because it's here, because of this body of believers united together through the years, that we still have these precious words: *now you are God's very own.*

Kogudus was started in Montana by an ALC Pastor, Olaf Magis. Pastor Olaf, as a young man during the war, was trying to escape to the free world. He was caught and imprisoned in a displaced persons' camp. It was during this time that the church, the organized church, gave him food and clothing and helped him get to America. He went to the seminary here and is now serving as a pastor at Glasgow, Montana. Kogudus has spread from Montana to Illinois, Minnesota, Idaho, the Dakotas, Oregon, Washington, and California with retreats being planned in Florida and Texas to take place, hopefully, this spring.

I went to a Kogudus in Urbana in January 1973. Kogudus was started for the men of the church, but because so many men who attended wanted their wives to share in this experience, about every third retreat is for women. My wife, Vicki, went to a women's Kogudus in March. I teach a Sunday school class of post high school young people and Vicki and I talked about the feasibility of a coed Kogudus for people in this age group. You only go to a Kogudus once, unless you go back to help lead one. I talked with Pastor Gene Peisker at St. Matthew in Urbana, who is in charge of Illinois Kogudus, and with Pastor Magis from Montana. They decided I should help with a men's Kogudus, and then go ahead with plans to have a young people's coed Kogudus as an experiment. We had no idea what would happen, but most of all we had no idea what God had in mind for us, and where in the course of one year he would take us. But I think most important of all, we had no idea the lives that would be changed along the way.

From the first youth Kogudus, a follow-up was started, sort of like a prayer group. We would meet every Friday evening at the church and talk about problems that came up during the week, and what Jesus had planned for our lives. It was at these share groups that it seemed as though the Lord was leading us to several people, young friends of those attending. Through much prayer and determination, they were able to convince one of their friends to attend a men's Kogudus in January. After he returned home, he thought a lot about what Jesus had done for him and started coming to church, and in February, he asked Pastor Spenn if he could be baptized. He wanted his life to be for Christ.

Then in February another young friend who happened to be a member of our church, though he hadn't attended for several years, was in trouble. Deep trouble—again. He was set to go back to prison. He had served eleven months in Vandalia for stealing drugs from a local doctor's office. After serving his time, he got out and was placed on probation, only to be involved in a car accident and charged with possession of a controlled substance. He had already at this time negotiated with the district attorney and had agreed to go back to prison for a one-to three-year term. He pleaded guilty and signed the papers.

We didn't want the young man back in prison. We couldn't do anything, but everything was possible with God. We turned everything in this matter over to Jesus and committed ourselves to doing, to the best of our ability, what the Lord wanted us to. Without going into detail, the end result was that in five days, this young man, after a suicide attempt, found his way to our home and moved in with us, and four days after that, he gave his life to Jesus Christ. Just two weeks later, after we appealed to the probation officer, the district attorney, and finally testified on his behalf at his trial, and prayed a lot, the judge dismissed the already signed negotiated plea of guilty and gave him four years probation. He was to stay and live with us for a while to see how things would go for him. This young man is still living with my wife and me and our four children today, and it looks like very shortly now, he's going to go on his own, and by the grace of God is a completely different person. He is now an usher in our church. *Once you were less than nothing, now . . .*

This past June, we got a letter from Pastor Olaf. In this letter he stated the chaplain at the Montana State Prison, who had himself been to a Kogudus, had asked for one at the prison for the inmates. Pastor Olaf said it might be a good opportunity if a team would volunteer. I knew just the guys. We prayed a lot about it for several days and decided that if the Lord wanted us to go, we would. It takes a lot of planning for Kogudus, and if we were to go, it needed to be before fall. Alan Klokkenga, one of the young men going, had one semester left at the University of Illinois, and shouldn't miss too much school, if possible. Owen Reiners was trying to get started in business for himself and Bob Eeten worked for him. They would have to take time off. I farm and really needed to be at home during harvest. So there wasn't much time to try and get things lined up. It was already July. By August 1 Pastor Magis called and said it was set up for Labor Day weekend, and if we would come, he and four others from Montana would meet us there. We would stay in the prison and eat with the inmates and sleep in the cells.

We would leave on the Wednesday morning before Labor Day weekend and try and get to Deer Lodge, Montana to the prison for a meeting Thursday night, about 1500 miles. We met with Pastor Spenn for a small communion prayer service at our church on Tuesday night. Kogudus friends and people from the church wrote prayer support letters to the inmates, and met in prayer for them on the Friday night during the Kogudus. Each inmate who was signed up to come was prayed for individually. The people from our community took up a collection to help us with our expenses and gave us $600. So Wednesday we were off with $600 and six hundred letters. What a blessing for so much support from our community and church.

Later, we received letters from some of the guys. Some came back to Christ, some made a first commitment, and some did nothing. We had prayed that if just one accepted Christ, it would be worthwhile. Wendilen Black, who had been in prison most of his life, wrote a letter to Vicki and me as we led a retreat for young people: "How thankful I am that there are people like you who care what happens to the lives of many sinners, and help keep them close to the Lord, as you have me. Had it not been for your help in our retreat here in prison, I do not know how long I would have continued a life full of hate and bitterness and sin. I hope and pray that Christ will speak through you to all the young people at this retreat as it did to me at ours. God bless both of you so dear. Your brother in Christ."

What has been God's purpose in all of this? I don't fully know. I'm sure all those young people at that first Youth Kogudus were a part. I'm sure the three young men who gave their lives to Christ and went to Montana with Vicki and I were a part, and the handful of new Christians in the prison, they surely must be a part, and now Camp Griesheim. What happens when men of the church work and plan together for one reason, to glorify Jesus Christ? Where do we go from here? I don't know. I think only God knows.

My reason for speaking to you this evening is in no way to tell you about the glorious Kogudus event, although, as I think you can see, it means very, very much to me, the versatility of it through the Gospel and the Church. Neither is it my idea to convince you to live as I do, because I falter and fall many times. I just wanted to share with you a part of my life and to try and impress upon you the wonderful love of Jesus Christ and the wonderful love and grace of God our Father, and to think once more, *"God has called you out of the darkness into his wonderful light. Once you were less than nothing, now you are God's own. Once you knew very little of God's kindness; now your very lives have been changed by it."*

"Timothy, oh Timothy, don't fail to do these things that God has entrusted to you." Timothy was a worker for God and for Paul. I think we can all be a "Timothy."

19

"Who Are We?"

St. Peter's Lutheran Church, Emden IL

Annual Brotherhood Supper, January, 1984

―――᎐ᨴ᎐᎐――――

As I think back on the good speakers that have been at the chili and oyster suppers, I'm sure your first question tonight is, "Why him?" I think I can explain that. Bud Westen called a couple of weeks ago and asked if I knew any speakers for the chili and oyster supper. I asked what kind he had in mind. He said there was only one prerequisite—he had to be cheap. Then he said, "How about you?"

I said, "Do I get my supper for free?"

He said, "No, you have to make a donation like everyone else."

I feel like I'm coming up in the world though, because the last place I spoke, they said they wouldn't ask me to speak there again if I paid them. Tonight all I have to do is pay for my supper. Leonard asked me a couple of times what I was going to talk about. I said, "I don't know."

I'd sure like to tell a joke on Leonard, but they told me the last time Bishop Osterbur met with some of the pastors, he told them they should refrain from telling ethnic jokes or jokes on specific people.

It didn't seem quite right. You know we tell jokes on the Polish people and on the Swedes. Bishop said if you want to tell a joke on someone or a group, choose something that will not offend, like a race of people that no longer exists. Well, I thought for a long time, and you know, in our Bethel class, in the Old Testament, we learned about the Hittites, and it seems they are mostly all gone; so I think I'll tell a Hittite story. There was this Hittite, and his name was Oly Leonard . . .

One of the greatest things that has happened to us lately is getting our new pastor and his wife, Joyce. Welcome, Pastor, to the annual Brotherhood Chili and Oyster Supper with the cheapest speaker on record.

You know, when Pastor got ready to come to Emden, one of the first things he sorted out was all his old sermons. He carefully put them in the corner of the basement so they wouldn't get lost or mixed up with the other items they were about to pack up. Well, one morning, just before they were to move, Pastor was shaving and he noticed it was really raining hard. All of a sudden he remembered those sermons in the corner of the basement and how sometimes it leaks in that corner of the basement when it rains so hard. Pastor almost panicked and he shouted for Joyce to run down and see about his sermons. Well, Joyce went down in the basement and came back up, and Pastor says, "Well, Joyce, were they wet? Are they okay?"

Joyce looked at him and said, "Don't worry, Pastor. They're just as dry as ever."

Harriet asked me Sunday morning after church what I was going to talk about, and I said, "Well, Harriet, I saw in the Lutheran Standard where the Brotherhood executive director, Luther Steinmeyer, said that Brotherhood members should prepare their organization's plans for 1984 around the theme, "Who are we?" And I said, "I guess you noticed Pastor Pieper used that as kind of a sub-topic." I said, "I guess maybe all great minds run together, but I've also heard if you leave fools alone long enough, they will finally congregate together." Harriet couldn't decide which was right. Harriet visited our Sunday school class Sunday morning and we sure did enjoy having her there.

Well, really, who are we? Here at St. Peter's, who are we? I John 3 says, "*See what love the Father has given us, that we should be called children of God; and so we are . . .*" I want to talk about St. Peter's and who we are, but I want to go back just a few years, at least far enough that I need to say not who are we, but who are you?

As most of you know, I wasn't born into St. Peter's. I wasn't a member until 1958. Let's take a quick poll. How many people here were baptized at St. Peter's? How many people's first home was more than ten miles from St. Peter's? How many men never heard of St. Peter's, but wanted some free chili? I was born about seven miles from St. Peter's, but never heard of it until they consolidated the grade schools. I went from the one-room Bethel school my first three years to Hartsburg in the fourth grade. It doesn't seem so far now, but then it seemed like it might just as well have been Peoria.

It was kind of strange the first time I heard St. Peter's mentioned. I remember exactly where I was. I was behind the Hartsburg Grade School talking to a boy in my grade. His name was Donald Jeckel. It was from him the first time I remember hearing the name St. Peter's. In case some of you don't know, Donald was a son of Marie Jeckel. Donald was sick a lot and walked with a limp because of a bone complication. I can't remember, but one of us asked the other where we went to church, and in the conversation, Donald said he went to St. Peter's. I asked him where it was and he said Emden. Then I remember he said, "You know Vicki Fink, don't you?" And I said no. The grade schools in Hartsburg and Emden were separate then, so the kids in Hartsburg didn't know many kids in Emden unless they went to church together. Well, Donald thought she was pretty cute and he told me he kind of liked her.

You know, Donald couldn't run as fast as the rest of us, and one day we were playing basketball outside. Donald was watching. The teacher came out of the door and shouted that she wanted to talk to me. I went over and she said to me, "Why don't you let Donald play on your team?"

Well, I didn't much want to because I wanted to win really bad, but I said, "Okay," and as I walked back past Donald, I said, "Come on, Donald, you be on my side."

Did you know the words, "Come on, Donald," were magic words? I didn't, but they were. Something pretty wonderful happened to me right then. I found out what it felt like to do something good for someone. I remember it was the best feeling I ever had in my life. I couldn't believe how he appreciated that. What a gift Donald had. Most of us don't know how to be appreciative when someone does something for us, but Donald did, and he made me feel terrific! That was my first experience I can remember of doing something for someone else.

It wasn't too long after that I had my first occasion to go to St. Peter's Church. I sat up in the balcony on the right side about the third row from the front. I remember crying. It was at Donald's funeral. I don't know, Marie, if you and your husband Harold taught Donald all that he gave to me, or if he was a natural, but I've often thought whatever desire I might ever have to help someone stemmed from knowing and loving Donald Jeckel. He also showed me that a life doesn't need to be long to be fulfilled, and oh, how I needed to know that when about twenty-eight years later I sat in St. Peter's at my own son's funeral.

As I got a little older, I ran across another member of St. Peter's. It was the one Donald had told me about—Vicki Fink. She turned out to be someone who had quite an impact on my life, and it was easy for me to see why he liked her. Vicki and I were married in August 1958. I had attended a little country church all my life—Presbyterian in Union. There were just a few members, so we all had a job. The doors were getting ready to close in about a year, so there was never any doubt that Vicki and I would go to "Vicki's" church. I was janitor and Sunday school superintendent and had voted in congregational matters since I was in high school. It was going to be different for me.

I wanted to belong to the church I was going to be married in, so I said my goodbyes that summer to Union Presbyterian and started adult instruction under Reverend Detjen. I was scared to death. I had never encountered so many people in church before. I thought, "They'll never accept me." Nevertheless, when Vicki and I were married, I was a member of St. Peter's. I thought, "A few years earlier I didn't know there was a St. Peter's and now I am one."

My first congregational meeting soon rolled around. Harold, Vicki's dad, took me. It was all men then, of course. Harold, by the way, was a great father-in-law. He always stood beside me, and whenever he said "okay," I could always get the credit. Well, anyway, I went to the meeting, came forward, and signed the constitution. I didn't know it, but I wasn't old enough. After I sat down, someone asked me my age and then a discussion started on whether to take my name off the books or leave it on, presuming someday I would be old enough. My fear of not being accepted seemed to be becoming a reality. I sank down lower and lower in my chair. Well, I lived through it, and not long after, John Boerma asked me to be a Sunday school teacher. That helped.

Somewhere in that time zone of years, another St. Peter's member, Elmer Krusemark, asked me to go to Iowa on a Harvestore tour. I went and that night, somewhere deep in Iowa, Elmer and I shared a room at a Holiday Inn. We talked a while about the tour and all the advantages of having a big blue glass-lined silo on the farm. Finally, I said, "I believe

I'll turn in," and he said, "Me too." Now, my light was the only one on in the room and when we got in bed, I turned it off. Right away Elmer's light came on. I thought he had to go to the bathroom or something. I kind of opened one eye and saw Elmer pick up a Gideon Bible and begin to read. That was a big thing to me—seeing a man two or three hundred miles away from home on a business trip taking time out to read the Bible before going to sleep.

It wasn't too long after that St. Peter's, St. John's and Immanuel decided to have a joint Sunday school teachers' workshop. It would meet once a week and have three classes, each taught by one of the three pastors. Vicki and I decided to go and enrolled in a class on the Holy Spirit taught by then—Pastor Osterbur. During the class, Bishop, or Pastor Osterbur, was talking about the Holy Spirit and salvation. When he asked the question, "How many of you know for sure you're going to heaven?" and he emphasized *for sure*, I thought, "That was a dumb question, no one knows for sure."

Lo and behold, Alma Cross, your daughter, Betty Ann, and, Marie Arnold, your daughter, Carol, raised their hands. I thought, "The nerve of those two." No one could be good enough to know for sure! It made me mad, and Vicki and I talked about it a big part of the night. I thought about it a long time and sometime after that, it started to sink in. Betty Ann and Carol had made me think we really can know for sure! Christ died for me that I might live!

Then along came Pastor Dryver. He asked me to be the Sunday school superintendent. Wow! That was pretty great! That proved I was accepted. Pastor Dryver then told me they had already asked twelve people and they had all declined, so they thought they should just as well try me. St. Peter's was teaching me humility.

In the early '70s, someone asked me to go to something called Kogudus. They said it meant Christian fellowship. I didn't like the sound of that at all. But Kogudus was a very special time. Among other things, it brought together for me what it seemed like so many of you already knew. It taught me to appreciate two things in particular: The Gospel, as it comes through the creed as taught in Luther's Small Catechism, and the church, the body of believers. I learned that in the church, the message must be proclaimed, heard, and passed on so that we might have fellowship with one another, and that the church must render service to others. Three things in the church must be emphasized: message, fellowship, and service. Of all things, the church is where it's at. The church is what has kept the good news of the Gospel alive all these years. The church is what Christ uses to "carry on."

In the fall of 1978, St. Peter's and this community taught me about caring for one another. Pastor Spenn and Leah taught me about getting ready when the times are good. It was that fall that Vicki and I stood by Tim's hospital bed and heard him say, "I think I'm going to die, but if I do, I know I'll go to heaven." How can you thank a church that puts the message into the minds of our young people? How do you thank a God that transfers that message from the mind to the heart and makes it real and personal? How do you thank St. Peter's and the community for caring for you when you can't care for yourself, for taking a part of your burden on themselves, for praying for you and loving you, and always, always showing you the love of Christ coming through themselves? The only way I know is to pass it on—like Pastor said Sunday, you spread his love to everyone, you want to pass it on.

We started out tonight with the topic "Who are we?" Then I changed it to "Who are you?" I feel I want to go back to "Who are we?" You can't treat me the way you have the last twenty-five and a half years without making me feel a part of St. Peter's and you. I know I'm a part. I've mentioned a few people's names tonight. I hope that's okay. Does that mean they might be better than someone else? By no means. They are what they are because of you—all of you from St. Peter's and this community.

I could go on and on with other names, but there is no end. I could tell about all those I've seen lose their spouses and be in church the next Sunday to worship and thank God for what they had and still have. I could tell you what Bob Cross taught me when he had his accident, or how Harold Marten gave a friend of mine a car on Sunday when his was broken down so he could go on home, a man he had never seen before. That man asked me later, "Why did he do that?"

All I could say was, "That's the way a lot of people are here."

Who are we? Did we turn this into a bragging and boasting evening on how good we are? I don't think so. Are my experiences here at St. Peter's so great? No, no more or less than yours. I've watched you—all of you—approach the communion rail, and I've heard Pastor and the deacon say, "*The body of Christ broken for you; the blood of Christ shed for you.*" I've seen you, on bended knees, reach out and take the bread and wine. I know you know your faults. I know you know your shortcomings. I hear you confess your sins and sing, "*Create in me a clean heart, O God.*"

Who are we? "*See what love the Father has given us that we should be called the children of God.*" I John 3:1. And so we are!

20

"Tell Your Children What You Believe"

Prayer Breakfast at Woodstock, Illinois

May 2, 1987

Good morning. It's great to be here this morning and be a part of your prayer breakfast. My wife, Vicki, and I drove up last night and stayed at the home of Everett and Francis Kuhns. We were made very comfortable and enjoyed their hospitality.

I woke up this morning and was wondering if anything I had to say was what God wanted me to say. I decided to pray about it. Now I don't know about you, but sometimes it's really hard for me to hear God. It felt to me that he was saying, "Just be yourself and don't say anything to offend or discourage anyone. These are my people and they have chosen to get up at five o'clock in the morning to meet here in prayer to honor me and to encourage one another. That's the important thing. You just tell them a little about yourself and your pilgrimage through life. They have chosen the essential."

Let me tell you a little about my life, and how in the world a down-state farmer could wind up being your speaker this morning. I'm a farmer from central Illinois—corn country. Are there any farmers here? Farming isn't very good right now. Corn and bean prices have fallen to half of what they were in the '70s and expenses are, of course, up. We started planting corn on April 20 and last week we had a little rain and I got in the house early that evening. Vicki had picked up a book for me and I stayed up till one o'clock reading it. The book was called, "*The Final Harvest*," written by Andrew Malcolm.

Mr. Malcolm works out of Chicago for the *New York Times* and has been following the developing farm crisis. In his book he describes a farm community in Minnesota, where a bankrupt small dairy farmer shot and killed the bank president, his chief loan officer, and later placed the barrel of a 12-gauge shotgun in his mouth and ended his own life. What a tragedy. Being a farmer, it was one of the most depressing books I have ever read, not just because of the killings, but because the events preceding them could be said about almost every farm community across the nation.

Farmers' dreams, in many cases, are dying and people are leaving the farm. We who farm in our area, central Illinois, are more fortunate than some. We have had two excellent crops, and although the prices are poor, most of us have had good enough yields to hang on. Andrew Malcolm wrote about the pressures of failure, in this case farming and small-town banking, but failure comes in all forms and shapes. I'll talk about some of them in a moment.

If I'm going to tell you a little about myself, I'll have to at least mention Kogudus. I attended a Kogudus retreat several years ago, and it was a big deal for me. It gave me time to reflect on what I believe and what's important to me, and what the church means to me. How can the church, or we as a caring community, be of help in time of failure?

Kogudus, by the way, is an Estonian word meaning "renewal," and was started by a Lutheran pastor, Olaf Magis from Montana. Pastor Magis grew up in Estonia and while he was still a young man, war broke out and the Nazi and Communist forces ran over the little country of Estonia. The people fled and Pastor Magis was captured and put into prison. Later, when the fighting worsened, they took them to the front lines. They ran again, hiding and running for days and ended up in a displaced persons' camp. While he was there, the organized church in America heard about them and reached out and helped him get to America where he could finish his education and become a Lutheran pastor.

Pastor Magis never forgot the caring community of the organized church, and because of this background, Kogudus was developed to help strengthen that community. It's been a real privilege for me to travel with Pastor Magis to other states to help new areas have Kogudus retreats. I've been to Florida, Oklahoma, Texas, Montana, Minnesota, and Wisconsin, to name a few, and Hawaii one January.

A couple of other things have come from Kogudus. People in our community who have attended Kogudus wanted to do something for the churches in our area, so we got together and formed Camp Griesheim Christian Retreat Center, Inc. We built a retreat center to have four or five Kogudus retreats a year, and rent it out the rest of the time to other churches and church groups. In 1985, we had our tenth anniversary, and to that date over thirteen thousand people had used the retreat center. It has been a real blessing working with all of those groups of people. We have a twelve-member board of which I am chairman and Vicki does all the scheduling.

Another little mission project of Kogudus has been the prison ministry. In 1974 the chaplain at Montana State prison, after attending a Kogudus retreat, asked for volunteers to try a Kogudus in prison. We found out about it and five of us from Illinois drove 1,600 miles to meet with Kogudus people in Montana for the first prison Kogudus. Since then, we have had over thirty prison retreats in Illinois, involving about one thousand inmates and many volunteers. We work with the prison chaplains, and even though we bring in the program, we assure them we are working for them and their ministry. It's been really exciting to watch people go in and minister to men in prison. Kogudus is a lay program under the guidance of a pastor. The whole retreat is done by lay people.

We talked earlier about failure. It's hard to describe the feeling of failure in the prison system. It is everywhere. How do you deal with a person who society says has failed so miserably that they have to be locked away from the rest of us? And how do you deal with a system that after men get out of prison, seventy to eighty percent of them return? Twenty to thirty percent of men incarcerated in the state of Illinois are illiterate. What chance is there for anything but failure in a high-tech world? We don't have enough money for education, yet it costs more to send a man to prison than it does to Harvard.

What's the answer? We build more prisons. Two have been built fifteen miles from my home in the last ten years and they continue to build. What is happening to us? I don't have any answers—I don't know. Why in the world would I want to talk about failure? Because we all have to deal with it in some form at some time. Failure—there are all forms. There are business failures, family relationship failures, people relationship failures, health failure, day-to-day failures.

When I was at Montana State prison, I met a young Indian there named Bo. I told him I cared for him and if he ever got out of prison to come and see me. I thought later I might have gotten carried away, but how could an Indian in prison in Montana, without a driver's license and no money, get to Illinois? Ha! I came home one evening and he was asleep on our sofa. He stayed eleven months. We had four children ages five to fifteen. It was a really interesting year. I was determined to be everything he never had. I failed miserably. I couldn't be that. I could talk to you for hours about this Indian and others who have lived with us, but we do not have the time this morning.

Failure—I think of my business failures. First off I'm a farmer. Would anybody like to buy a garbage compactor that compacts garbage a semi load at a time in Greeley, Colorado? Boy, could I make you a deal on that. Or there was the time I bought a farm in Missouri, kept it a couple of years, and sold it for a $25,000 profit. Not much maybe, but it was the first time I ever made any money without working. The only catch—I sold it to a man who was a farmer and also the chief executive officer of the Bucklin State Bank in Bucklin, Missouri, and took a second mortgage on $25,000, my profit. Everyone assured me it was fine, but the third year I didn't receive a payment, so I called out to the bank and found I was talking to a lady from the Federal Deposit Insurance Corporation. The bank was closed and the chief officer was gone; they thought maybe he went to California.

One other time I bought thirty thousand bushels of corn on the board of trade. Jimmy Carter didn't like what Russia was doing and placed an embargo against them. Corn prices plummeted for two weeks. Failure. I wanted to be the perfect husband and father, but like Bo the Indian, you can't be everything to someone—that's God's job. It's just so hard to learn that.

I can remember a little over eight years ago things were going pretty good. It was 1978 and I was about two-thirds through a good harvest. Inflation was booming—easy to pay off old debts. We were traveling quite a bit with Kogudus and with prison retreats, and lots of church work. We had been really involved with Kogudus and the church for five years. Vicki and I made a decision we weren't going to play church anymore. We were going to get serious. We felt we had at least some kind of an intimate relationship with Jesus Christ and we wanted it to grow. Now I'm in no way telling you that, because that's where we were (and still are), that you should be there. I'm simply telling you where I am.

Jesus himself said, "*In my Father's House are many rooms; I go to prepare a place for you.*" I don't believe we fully understand what he means here. Could it be there are many places for many people who some of us may be surprised to see there? I don't know. Anyway, Vicki and I made a decision to dedicate our children to the "glory of God." They were his—he gave them to us. So one night we knelt beside the bed and stumbled through a prayer telling Christ we were entrusting them to his care.

Not long after that I was combining corn and Vicki brought Todd and Tim to the field. Todd was sixteen, Tim fourteen. They wanted to work after school. I told them to go to another farm about six miles away to plow. They took Vicki home and headed to the field in the van. About four miles down the road, they went off the road and then turned over in a field. When Vicki and I got there, Todd was walking around. He was okay, but Tim had been thrown through the windshield and the van had rolled over him. He was struggling to breathe. We were kneeling on the ground beside him, and Vicki said as she looked across the field, she kept hearing in her mind, "*This is not unto death, but for the glory of God.*"

The ambulance soon came and took him to Lincoln Hospital. In Lincoln they sent him on to Springfield and took him into surgery. The surgery lasted six hours—he had a ruptured esophagus. After the surgery he couldn't eat or drink and couldn't talk because of the tube in his throat, but he kept his spirits up and was focused on his recovery because he wanted to get back to playing basketball.

A little over a week later they moved him out of intensive care and he could whisper some words to us, but he soon had a setback and they took him back into intensive care. We could not stay in there with him and very early the next morning the nurses came out and said they had called the doctor and he was going to operate again. I went in to Tim and he whispered, "I've been praying all night. I think I'm going to die, but I'm not afraid. I know I'm going to heaven." During his surgery we stayed in the chapel. Some friends and family started to arrive and we all prayed together.

After finishing our prayer, we looked up and the doctor was standing by the door. He came in and said, "We lost him."

I said, "I want to see him."

The doctor said, "He's still your son; he always will be your son."

When we arrived back home I went upstairs to his room and laid on his bed. I felt like the *ultimate failure*. I didn't even get my son raised. I cried—I felt like I was going to throw up—and then I felt God's presence and it was like he asked, "What did you want for Tim? Really?" And I thought, "To know you and that maybe he could tell someone else about you, but now I just want him . . ." and all of a sudden it hit me! *I was not a failure*. I had a child in heaven.

We had a memorial service and our pastor let me give the message. It was for Tim's friends. I told them what Tim had said and what he relied on when everything else failed. Not friends, not basketball, not even me. He relied on Christ. I told them about seeing him right after he died and that it was like an old coat. Tim's message was brought to his friends. I got to be the spokesman for him and God.

My prayer for at least one of my children has been answered: that he know God and is able to tell others about him. Vicki's Bible verse was true. *This is not unto death, but for the Glory of God.* Not the way we thought God meant it, but nevertheless true. And lest I forget it, I had the stone-cutter cut those words in marble on Tim's tombstone. *This is not unto death, but for the Glory of God.*

Good people in Woodstock, we have a God so great that he can use our failures, not only for his purposes, but to make us more like the kind of person we want to be. Isn't that something! All things do work for good for those who love God. Do I have any closing advice? Maybe just one thing to consider: tell your children what you believe whether they are five or fifty-five. It will help them to know what they believe. Why is that? I don't know, but they are a part of us, and they need to know.

Thank you for having me here. I want to thank my friend, Don Johnson, for recommending me to Mrs. Kuhns and the rest of the committee. Please know that I will never forget this day and what it has meant to me to be here.

21

"Two Treasures"

St. Peter's LYO Supper & Program

2002

John Cross wanted to know if I'd tell a story, and I said, "Well, I'm not very good at stories. I don't know very many." But, you know, in the lower level of our house, we've got a room, and for lack of a better word, I call it my office. And in that room, I can do anything I want to do. If I get it dirty, it stays dirty, unless I can talk somebody into cleaning it, 'cause it's mine. I've got a lot of stuff in there and over in the corner of that room, I've got a two-by-three foot framed picture of Jesus Christ that the chaplain of Montana State Prison gave to me. It means a lot to me. Right in front of that, I've got a cross that Owen Reiners made for me about twenty-five years ago. So that's a really special place for me. And once in a while, depending on how things are going, maybe really good or maybe really bad, I'll sit down there and look at that picture and that cross a while and think about what life is all about.

The other day I was sitting down there and I was thinking about this guy. He walked into church on a Sunday morning, and as he walked into the church, he noticed that up in the front of the church there was a group of young people. They were singing and people were leading them. And as he went on through the church, he saw kids going to Sunday school, and he saw teachers coming in to help them get their coats off and get their Bibles out.

So, he went back in his thoughts and he walked through the church again. And when he saw the group up in front who were practicing for the service, he noticed there was a lady at the piano who was playing for them, and he noticed a couple of other people running around getting things together for them.

There were three or four older people in the choir too, and he said, "They've got a lot of talent," like Jane Mikelson who plays the piano; Sandy Goeken and Carol Reiners, who help the young people get these things together; the Sunday school teachers, who teach the young ones upstairs; Tom, who teaches the high school class; and John, who works so hard with the kids.

Later, he went to the church service, and low and behold, the young people were leading the whole service, and he thought, "This church is a church with two treasures: a treasure of young people, and a treasure of older people who are willing to help."

Well, the guy I'm telling you about who was walking through that church is me. The church with the two treasures is St. Peter's, because we've got a whole bunch of kids, and there are a lot of people who are willing to help them. And for the people who can't help them, they give money and applause and pray for them so they can go to Chicago and be with other kids, all learning to know more about Jesus Christ.

I noticed too, that this church didn't have a regulation pastor, and they were so worried. But then you know what God did for that church? He gave them two pastors. Yes, I'm talking about St. Peter's all right. We've got Pastor Pieper and we've got Pastor Jay. We've got someone to call on shut-ins and we've got another pastor who will sit with the kids and teach them how to pray. That church is a church with two treasures.

As I sit in my office thinking about all of that, sitting in front of the cross that Owen made me, well, every once in a while, depending on if things are going really good or really bad, I'll sit and pray a moment, and if nobody's around, I'll sing a song.

Now I'd like to sing a song here tonight that I haven't played or sung for a long time. I quit because I wasn't any good. But I'm going to play anyway, and I want you to sing the chorus with me. I want you to think about the church with two treasures, because you're one of those treasures. You're either one of the young people or one of those who are not so young. We've got two treasures here, and no one is excluded.

> In moments like these I sing out a song,
> I sing out a love song for Jesus.
> In moments like these I sing out a song,
> I sing out a song to the Lord:
> Singing, I love you, Lord.
> Singing, I love you, Lord.
> Singing, I love you, Lord.
> I love you.

In moments like these I sing out a song,
I sing out a love song for Jesus.
In moments like these I lift up my eyes,
I lift up my eyes to the Lord:
Singing, I love you, Lord.
Singing, I love you, Lord.
Singing, I love you, Lord.
I love you.

Part III

Prison Ministry and Retreats

---

22. "What Do You Believe?"—Menard, March 2, 1979, and Vandalia, June 10, 1979 135
23. "How Love Changes Us"—Dwight Prison 139
24. "Alone with Jesus"—Kogudus Keystone Meditation, March 1979 143
25. "Sharing the Love of Christ with Those Who Are Hurting"—WELCA-ECC, March 11, 1989 147
26. "Jesus Loves Me"—First English Lutheran, Peoria / Gifford, February, 1990 155
27. "Ministry in Daily Life"—Lutheran Men In Mission, NE Conference, September 15, 1990 163
28. "We Are Where We Are so Christ Can Be There"— Macon, Missouri, December 9, 1990 167
29. "God's Grace for All"—Criminal Justice Week, Presbyterian Church 171

22

"What Do You Believe?"

Menard Prison—March 2, 1979

Vandalia Prison—June 10, 1979

———~~~◦◦◦~~~———

(Jerry gave this talk at weekend Kogudus Prison Retreats in which the talks are based on the Apostles' Creed.)

Last night we talked about listening to God and to one another. Today we will be talking about something called the Apostles' Creed. There will be several talks today dealing with the different parts of the Apostles Creed, namely the Third Article, the First Article, and the Second Article. What this simply means is the Creed is broken up into three different parts, and there is a talk on each of these parts.

Why in this Kogudus do we use the Apostles' Creed? In many of the churches, the Apostles' Creed is spoken every Sunday morning, but in others, it isn't. Now this certainly isn't to say that those who don't use the Creed are wrong. Not at all. It's just to say that many people feel the Creed is an important way of expressing one's faith. It should be noted that the Creed is not certain scriptures, but we feel it is sort of a summary of scripture.

Okay, once more, why the Creed? Read Matthew 10:32 and 33. This is entitled, "*Confessing and Rejecting Christ.*" It seems as though Jesus is asking here for a declaration of faith. In other words, we could say he is asking for a faith that is expressed, declared or confessed (spoken).

In Philippians 2:9-11, it seems we are asked to make a confession of faith. We are kind of put on the spot, and the question is *"What do you believe?"* The Apostles' Creed is the oldest form for a confession of the Christian faith. It has survived many years of struggles and tests, and comes to us as a summary of biblical revelation.

Let's read the Creed together. Please note the three parts it is divided into. These are what the rest of the talks I was telling you about will be on later today. Look at the words and think about them as you read them. The Creed has been used by many churches for years. The word "*creed*" means "*I believe.*" So when we talk about the Creed, we talk about a statement of faith, a summary of what Christians believe.

This little talk has two parts. In the first part, we talk about the statement and the history of that statement of the Creed itself. In the second part, we will talk about the faith and what is essential about faith.

What is the history of the Apostles' Creed? They say the Creed has been used in a very similar way within one hundred years after Jesus himself walked on earth. Our Creed is called the Apostles' Creed because it summarizes the teachings of the apostles. It reaches a long way back. When we repeat this Creed, we are saying something that the church has used to express its faith for almost two thousand years. When we repeat this Creed, we can feel that we are a part of a living body of God's people, reaching out not only to all parts of the world now, but also reaching out into the past, the present, and the future of God's people. God's family is eternal.

It is said, though it may just be a legend, that after Jesus was raised from the dead and ascended into heaven, and after Pentecost when the Holy Spirit came and the disciples were able to talk in different languages, the Lord commanded them to go out and preach the Word of Jesus. So before they left each other and parted company, they got together a statement they all agreed to use as a common form of teaching. As I said, this may be a legend, but it points out the need we and the disciples have for a common form for teaching and preaching.

Another reason for the need for a creed was false teachers. Just as today, all kinds of people from all kinds of places became Christians and started putting their own ideas into their preaching. Pretty soon, there were all kinds of ideas and preaching going around. The Creed came about from these needs and situations of the early church. But the question was and still is, "*What do we believe?*"

Where does faith come in? What is essential to faith? Does it have to do with reason or emotion, understanding, feelings or experience? What is it? Isaiah 1:18 says, "*Come let us reason.*" This does not say we can think our way to heaven, but what God says to us in his word must involve our thinking, our reasoning, and our studying. "*Come let us reason together,*" says the Lord.

Well, what then is essential in faith? Is it reason or emotion? They are both important. One is not complete without the other. Sometimes we try to make the Christian faith reasonable. We are tempted to leave out the mysterious and the unexplainable, and by doing this, we have starved one part of man, the part that knows there is more to life than what can be put under the microscope.

There seems to be a need to experience. There is sometimes a vacuum in this lonely world of lonely people. If this is true, is it possible we are going too far the other way? If we are going to be open to experience, we will be open not only to the Holy Spirit, but also to the spirit of man and of Satan. Horoscopes are in our papers. Mysticism and superstition are no longer bad words in our space age. Remember, experiences must be tested. *"Come let us reason together,"* says the Lord.

So then what is essential to faith? Faith is more than reason. Faith is more than experience. Faith is more than reason and experience. Faith is a gift from God. It is a mystery and a gift. Let's look at faith from another angle. What is faith? (Hebrews 11:1) A complete definition of faith is impossible, but we know it takes trust. We have faith in Jesus Christ. One of the dangers for us as Christians is that we think we know it all. We sit back and discuss all kinds of theories on Christianity instead of bowing down before the wounds of Christ, instead of taking our shoes off our feet, because the place on which we stand is holy ground. We can discuss faith from all angles, but what makes faith meaningful is what we have faith in—Christ.

It's not me, not you, not Billy, not Hank, not Rowley, not Roger, not these guys who come along with me. It's Jesus. It's all grace. It's all him. Even the Holy Spirit doesn't point to his own works, but his work is to point to Jesus and what he has done for us. Faith means looking to Jesus. Faith does not point to itself, but to Jesus. If you should die today, what will happen to you? Will you go to heaven? Why should God let you in? Because of what Jesus has done for us all.

23

"How Love Changes Us"

Dwight Prison, Dwight, IL

Our theme today is "How Love Changes Us." As I think about that, I'm not sure. I know most people give you facts. I don't have many facts, except a little scripture. I just want you to consider what it means—what love is—real love. I mean *real* love. I've been able to travel—Florida, Texas, Montana, Niagara Falls, Washington, D.C., Hawaii—to the top of the Continental Divide in Glacier National Park and the bottom of the Grand Canyon, and I haven't found it. I haven't found real love anywhere—not real love, but I found where it's at. It's at Jesus.

I've found where it's at and I'm struggling to get to it. It is Jesus, the only person who really loves. No one else really loves me. I can ask others. They say, "Yes, I love you," but they let me down, my friends and family. In prison we learn to do right or the law will get you. Outside we say better follow the law or we'll fall, and that's right. Man has set up laws and if we don't conform, in the slammer you go. We become so engrossed in the law of God, the Ten Commandments, and man that we miss the love of Jesus.

Someone hasn't shown us the love. And I can't show it to you either, but I can tell you where it's at. Someone hasn't shown us Jesus—not really—not enough to see his love. Because if we knew his love, really knew it, what need would there be for the law? Jesus said I didn't come to do away with the law, but to fulfill it—in you and me. You love, he says, and I'll take care of the law. I mean *really love*. I don't know how to show you his love. I don't know how to make it real to you. I can't. All I can do is show you a person who said I will die for your sin—because I love you too much to let you die for it.

Now this law, the Ten Commandments—what Jesus is saying is forget the law. Now wait before you all start scaling the fences! Jesus is saying concentrate on me and the love that I have for you, because to concentrate and think only of the law and its punishment creates what? Hate, not love, but hate. Hate for ourselves, hate for those around us, even hate for God. It's too hard to follow. It's impossible to follow this law, any part of it, without love. So then we say, okay, give me some. I'm tired of this, so you turn to Jesus, get a big batch of love, and later a big batch of booze, and back in the slammer. So what good is love? What good is the law?

Draw closer to the love—we aren't close enough yet. Get closer to Jesus. Follow him. Trust him. We don't trust him because we don't know him. Get closer to Jesus. How? Go in whatever way you can. Read, talk, anything. The only way for me is to lay and think, because first in my mind it has to be what I want. Read about him a little. Find out who he is and think about it. No matter what happens, he loves us. Draw closer to him. He's our only salvation in this world and our salvation in the next.

How does love change us? It brings us closer to him—Jesus—and that is the goal. Love changes us to want to be closer to it. If Jesus is that great, why is he going to mess around with you and me? You know why. You want to know why? Because he's already in us. We just don't know it or fully realize it. I'm convinced that everyone breathing has somewhere within himself the Spirit of Christ. If you're breathing, Christ loves you. And if you stop breathing—well, he loves you even more.

Love will change us, because it's *real* love. To rely on the law results in failure and we are done for. But to rely on love—to fail then is not failure because Jesus says I'll take that, I love you. Yes, we will have to suffer the consequence of man's law if we fail—we can't get around that—but we have not failed Jesus because of his love.

I wish I could tell you I love you that way, but that would be wrong; I would fail you. But I can tell you Jesus loves you. He's already there inside of us telling us, "*I love you.*" May we all soon realize it.

24

"Alone with Jesus"

Kogudus Keystone Meditation

March 1979

Christ calls us to fellowship in the community and to fellowship alone with him. Christ desires both. Tonight, according to our agenda, we are to visit here in the fellowship of this community of Kogudus leaders about being alone, fellowshipping alone with Christ.

Dietrich Bonhoeffer, in his book, *Life Together*, talks about being alone with God. He quotes Luther as Luther talked about death, saying, "Everyone must fight his own battle with death, by himself, alone. Yet even in death you are not alone, and on the last day you will be one member of the great congregation of Jesus Christ."

So what does it mean to be alone with Jesus? Bonhoeffer says our day needs definite times of silence, silence under the word and silence that comes out of the word. This, I guess, is meditation. Let me share with you a few personal thoughts on meditation and prayer.

Meditation can be called listening to God. There are many ways of listening to Jesus. I would like to narrow this down to a word we are using this weekend: "Encounter." Encounter means to be face to face. Face to face with Jesus.

In I Kings 19 we read, *"Go forth, and stand upon the mount before the Lord."* In Luke 24 we read about the Emmaus road experience and how Jesus interpreted the scriptures to the disciples. In verse 32 they said to each other, *"Did not our hearts burn within us while He talked to us on the road, while He opened to us the Scriptures?"*

I am of the opinion that if we would meditate, be in solitude and silence under the word, have a daily, face-to-face encounter with Jesus Christ, then this world would be different. I believe that with all my heart. I know Jesus can use our mistakes and our shortcomings. I also know that no matter what we do, he can't love us any more than he does right now. But I believe with all my heart that this world would be different if we had a daily encounter with Jesus.

This week on television, some of us saw parts of the Martin Luther King story. At one time he said, "To really carry out the precepts of Jesus would be the most revolutionary and dangerous thing in the world." What would happen if we did? We really don't know, except that every move we made would be in love and understanding.

What makes it possible to follow the precepts of Jesus? It is silence under the word, meditation, an encounter with Jesus. It is being face to face with him. I believe that's what the difference was that made men like Martin Luther and Martin Luther King Jr. do what they did.

I'm not saying God is calling us to be like those men, but I believe that's what made those men great. They were great because they were silent under the word in an encounter with Jesus. Elijah could stand anything except the still, small whisper of God. When Jesus opened the scriptures to the two on the Emmaus road, their hearts burned within them.

Dr. King said, "I have been to the mountain. I don't care what happens to me anymore. I have been to the mountain. I have seen the Promised Land." He didn't mean he could see the black man's freedom soon. He didn't mean he could see the rewards of his work. What I think he meant was he had stood in silence under the word while Jesus opened the scriptures. He no longer cared what happened to him. He had been to the mountain.

We are quick to read our Bibles and our daily devotions. We might run to visit the sick or our brother in prison or listen intently to someone pouring out his problems, and this is what we should do. But can we come face to face with Jesus, alone? Can we step from our comfortable life and take his hand and let him tell us the word of love, giving, suffering, humiliating love?

Do I believe all this? Yes, I believe it. I believe it so much that I'm afraid to do it. If I didn't believe it, I could do it easy. But since I believe it, it kind of scares me because to follow the precepts of Jesus, to encounter him alone, to let him tell us about the word of love and truth, would be the most dangerous and revolutionary thing in the world. Why? Because every day our life would be renewed. The promises he gave us through our baptism would come to light. We would be changed.

Meditate, be silent under the word, come face to face with Jesus, and prayer will follow. *"Seek first the Kingdom of God, and all these things will be added to you."* Seek him through meditation.

At the beginning of this article, I quoted Luther as saying that everyone must fight his own battle with death by himself, alone. Yet even in death, you are not alone. Little did I realize last February that eight months later, I would witness our fourteen-year-old son fight his own battle with death. Little did I realize what it would be like to watch "one of our own" encounter Jesus face to face by himself, alone.

Tim was injured in a van accident on October 19. He lived eleven days in St. John's Hospital in Springfield, Illinois. At 1:00 in the morning on Saturday the 28, I left his room. I came back at 5:00 a.m. He told me he hadn't slept but had been praying all night. He asked me to pray with him, and I did.

Solitude and silence. Tim found out what it was all about, being face to face with Jesus. He told us he thought he was going to die, but that he wasn't afraid. He said he knew he was going to heaven.

We received cards and letters and telephone calls from people all over the country. They were praying with us for Tim. Everyone really did care. Never before had I been able to experience the "caring community" in such a real way.

Tim fought for the life he loved clear to the end. His life of many friends, motorcycles, and basketball was so important to him. He left here on October 30 when his heart stopped, and he went on to something better. He went to be with the one he had heard about in Sunday school, church, and confirmation, the one who became so real to him during the solitude and silence of those last eleven days.

How was Tim able to be willing to give up this life he loved so much? It was through what the church had taught him and what he had in his mind when it became a reality as it transferred from his mind to his heart. The church, the caring community, became very real to us all, and we are most grateful.

"This illness is not unto death; it is for the glory of God . . ." (John 11:4) *"Now to him who by the power at work within us is able to do far more abundantly than all that we ask or think, to him be glory in the church and in Christ Jesus . . ."* (Ephesians 3:20-21).

25

"Sharing the Love of Christ With Those Who are Hurting"

Women of the ELCA—East Central Conf.

March 11, 1989

Good morning. My name is Jerry Crane and I'm here to visit with you about Justice Ministries. Some of you have been planning and working a long time for today. Sharon Hovelin called me a couple of months ago getting things lined up. Others of you have put aside important jobs or engagements to be here today. You all got up early, got ready, got in your car, or caught a ride with someone else to make the trip here. And long or short, it was an effort, but you are here.

I believe you have a right to wonder why I'm here. I would if I were you. Whenever I go to a meeting and I don't know the speaker, I always wonder why him—or her? What can she or he have to tell me?

The last few years I have been involved with a type of prison ministry. I guess that's the bottom line of why me—and I'd simply like to share some of those last few years with you and maybe a couple of ways you or your group could be involved.

First let me see where you people are from. I have a hard time trying to get these areas straightened out in my mind. This is the Central Eastern Conference, right? And you're in the Central Southern Synod. Okay, what's the furthest point north, south, east, west? How many of you are now or have been involved with agriculture? Since I'm a farmer I kind of wondered about that.

I guess I'd like to tell you about my family. Vicki is with us today. We have four children: Todd—he works with me and within the last year has become a Country Companies insurance agent. My second, Tim, is deceased. Tonya, my oldest daughter, is attending ICC Junior College in Peoria, and Tasha is a senior in high school planning on college this fall. I have two grandchildren.

If I'm going to visit with you about Justice Ministries, or in my case, about prisons, I'm going to have to go back a few years when an acquaintance of mine asked me to go to a retreat called Kogudus. It was going to be held at Urbana over semester break at a Lutheran fraternity.

Now before I go any further, I feel like I have to tell you that all this stuff I'm going to talk about today is kind of my story. Everybody has a story and my story isn't a bit better than your story, but it's the only one I know. I'm not saying it's been good or bad—I don't know—but whatever, it's a part of my story.

Back to this retreat called Kogudus. I couldn't decide if I wanted to go or not, but Vicki and I finally decided it would be okay. Vicki just said, "Be sure and don't get involved." If I told you that Kogudus didn't change anything for me, I wouldn't be telling you the truth. It changed the way I looked at Jesus Christ, the way I looked at the church, and it changed the way I looked at those around me, not because I heard anything different—it was all things I had heard before—yet it all seemed to make sense and fall a little more into place for me, what the church had been telling me all along.

Basically, Kogudus is just a short course in Christianity as the Lutheran Church teaches. I learned that it didn't really matter who I am, but whose I am, and that God had used the church to keep his word and sacraments alive all these years, and I was a part of that church, the body of believers, the caring community. Isn't that something?!

Soon after I went to Kogudus, Vicki went to one for women. We were teaching a Sunday school class for post-high school and college-age students. We convinced the national director of Kogudus, a Lutheran pastor from Montana, to let us try a Youth Kogudus for young men and women together using the same program. That was in 1973 and there has been a youth Kogudus every summer since then. Many of these people are leaders in our church and other churches today.

What's this have to do with prison? A friend of these young people had become involved with drugs and had robbed a doctor's office, and been sent to prison for four years. I wrote to him while he was in prison, but he didn't respond. He served one year and was paroled, but very soon violated his parole, and the judge said he would have to go back to prison and finish out the remainder of his original sentence—another three years. Vicki and I went to see his parole officer and convinced him that it might be better if Bob—that was his name—could live with us instead of going back to jail. The judge gave his permission.

We had four kids at home then, ages three to twelve, but it worked out really well. Bob went to Kogudus while he lived with us and even helped on a Kogudus team that summer. While he was here we got a newsletter from the national Kogudus office. In it was an article written by a Lutheran prison chaplain from Deer Lodge, Montana. He had attended a Kogudus and was wondering about having one for some of his men in prison. He was asking for volunteers.

On Labor Day weekend, five of us—Bob Eeten, Alan Klokkenga, Owen Reiners, Vicki, and myself—drove 1,600 miles to Deer Lodge, Montana, for the first prison Kogudus. We met several other volunteers there. It, too, was quite a weekend. It was the first time I had ever been in a prison. We slept in the cells. It was an old maximum-security prison where the guards still walked on the tops of the walls. There were quite a few Indians in prison in Montana, and one in particular, I told before we left, "Bo, if you ever get out of prison, come and see us." That was pretty easy. How could an Indian with no driver's license and no money get all the way from Montana to Illinois? Ha! I came home one evening and he was asleep on our sofa. He stayed eleven months. Our children were five to fifteen then.

I could talk eleven days about those eleven months, but after some very tall stories and some dangerous actions, we finally told him he would have to leave. He left and ended up back in prison for a couple of years.

One day I received a message to contact the Lutheran chaplain at Menard Correctional Center. We drove to Menard at Chester, Illinois, and a couple of months later had the first prison Kogudus in Illinois. That was in 1977. After that we went to Vandalia. We've since been to Dwight, Hillsboro, Centralia, Lincoln, Danville, and Vienna. We also went to Wisconsin to help get Kogudus started there, and a couple of years later returned to help them with their first prison Kogudus. We have had over thirty-five prison retreats now in Illinois involving well over a thousand inmates and volunteers from the outside.

Why am I telling you all of this? A couple of reasons: to tell you how I got into prison ministry, and to tell you that we had a fairly large group of people who had been to Kogudus. Some wanted to be involved in prisons. Some said no way—that's not for me. So the prison ministry became sort of a mission project for Kogudus, and those who wanted could be as involved as they wanted to, and those who didn't—that was okay. There's a lot of other ways to serve, and for those who did get involved, it was only to the extent they felt comfortable.

Some want to go into the prisons for a weekend and sit with inmates and share their faith and listen to them. Others say no, but I will write letters or give prayer support, or help with finances. It's not wrong to draw a line and say this I will do and this I won't. You don't have to let ex-offenders move in with you and your family, or give them money. Many times that's exactly the wrong thing to do. All we are asked to do is to share the love of Christ with those who are hurting. You decide what you are comfortable with. If we don't reach out—who will? We can't expect the state to.

When we first started going to prisons there was a state chaplain with an office in Springfield. He coordinated programs and handled problems with all of the prison chaplains. That job is no more. There is now no state chaplain, and many chaplains that move or retire are not being replaced. Maybe this shouldn't be—I don't know. Maybe it's the job of the church, like how we send missionaries. I honestly don't know.

How big is the need? According to a CBS special about prisons on TV this year, there are over, and I quote, "one million people locked behind bars and fences in the United States." They went on to say, "That will increase by fifty percent by the next century-eleven years. U.S. prisons have doubled in the last decade. Prison population has grown five times as much as the crime rate. Most states are under court order to build new prisons. President Bush will need to spend five billion dollars on new federal prisons alone."

Let's get a little closer to home. There are twenty thousand people incarcerated in the state of Illinois. It costs more to send a man to prison than it does to send him to Harvard University. Seventy percent or more of people in prison end up going back. There are over two thousand men locked up at Menard—one half have no jobs at all. Over six hundred men have signed themselves into PC, protective custody, because they fear for their safety—gangs, stabbings, rape.

We have nineteen adult correctional centers in Illinois, five work camps, fourteen community correctional centers, six youth centers, and then all the county jails. And of all the people locked up, according to CBS, seventy-five percent are locked up because of alcohol or drug-related crimes, and they are locked together with hard-core criminals.

What's a better way? I don't know, but if we are Christian people whose job is to reach out to those in need, we've got a problem here—or an opportunity!

Let's talk about women inmates. There are over eight hundred women incarcerated in the state of Illinois: over seven hundred and fifty in Dwight and over seventy-five in Logan at Lincoln. What are some of the problems here? What about the children? Can you imagine what it means for children to be separated from their mothers? Lutheran Social Services has started a program called the Dwight Project. It is designed to reconnect mothers in Dwight with their children using volunteers who will transport the children to Dwight on a regular basis for visits.

You may have read about the camp-outs at Dwight last summer. The women who had qualified with good behavior were given the use of a tent on the grounds at Dwight and their children could come and stay with them for the weekend. It was a great success, but some kids didn't show up because there was no one who would or could bring them. What about the children? It's not their fault, but they still are hurt.

Some of you may have a spouse or a family member who has been, or is, in prison. If no one from the church reached out to you, I am sorry. We, in the caring community, have sometimes failed in some places. Prisons could be one of those places. But those people are hard and calloused, we say—what do they know about feelings and what about the feelings of those they hurt? What do they deserve anyway?

Let me tell you a story. Our son, Tim, died as a result of an automobile accident at the age of fourteen. He seemed to be recovering, but had a setback and was going to need surgery again. That morning I went in to see Tim and he whispered, "I've been praying all night. I think I'm going to die, but I'm not afraid. I know I'm going to heaven." Nothing else mattered except saying *"yes"* to Jesus Christ.

Do those in prison deserve the same chance as Tim did to know Christ? They have the same Savior as everyone else. But what about those feelings of people in prison I mentioned before I started this story? Several days after Tim's funeral, I received a short note from an inmate from Menard. He had been locked up for ten years. He had heard about Tim's death and sent the note expressing his sympathy and said he would pray for me and my family. At the end he said something I hope I will never forget. He said, "Today I prayed that God would let me die before you, and no matter what far corner of heaven I might be in on the day that you die, that God would call me to be there to witness you and Tim reunited once more." What a compassionate thought that was for me.

I've talked a lot about caring and compassion. Is there another side? Yes, the victim and his pain. That is justice ministry too. Who are we that go to church and raise our families and pay our bills the best that we can? What can we do with such a massive problem? Let me offer a few suggestions. If you don't already have one, form some kind of justice ministry group in your conference or synod. Everyone who is interested could be a part. Remember, you don't have to, but there is something everyone can do who wants to.

Contact Lutheran Social Services of Illinois. They have an active justice ministry, but they need help. Here's a couple of things: the Dwight Project I talked about earlier, LSSI will help you get started with this.

Orientation is offered to help you prepare. There are also brochures from Companions. Besides the Dwight Project, Companions has things for groups or individuals to do: write letters, send birthday or Christmas cards, make cookies. This might be something kids could do. Pick up one of their newsletters.

Also, it's a long way to southern Illinois prisons from Chicago. Many people cannot afford gas money or bus fare and overnight lodging. A hospitality house has been opened in Chester just a few blocks from Menard Prison. The first year over two thousand guests stayed for donations only. They need support, and more hospitality homes are needed. One is needed in the Vienna area now. Call LSSI if you want to be involved.

Last Sunday, the Gospel was Luke 15:11-31 about the prodigal son. Who are we? Are we the prodigal son or are we the son who wasn't interested in his brother coming home again? I wish it was that simple. Of course, we are sometimes the prodigal son who runs away from God, but are we sometimes the son who isn't interested in his brother coming home, even though he's alone and in prison?

It's almost Easter. There are a lot of people out there who need to be welcomed home by the caring community. Jesus hung on the cross so there could be no doubt. He wants us all to come home. Amen.

26

"Jesus Loves Me"

First English Lutheran, Peoria, IL

St. Paul Lutheran, Gifford, IL

February, 1990

I'm certainly glad to be with all of you here for Prison Ministry Sunday. Normally, I would be sitting in a pew this morning at St. Peter's Lutheran Church in Emden. I'm a farmer. My wife, Vicki, who is with me this morning, and I, and one daughter still at home, live on the farm near Hartsburg, which is close to Emden where we go to church.

Peoria is becoming a household word at our house. We have two daughters going to ICC this year, and Vicki very soon will be working in Peoria. She works for Lincoln Office Environments and their new owner is moving the corporate office from Lincoln to Peoria to a brand-new building out on Knoxville just south of Pioneer Parkway. I'm sure it's going to be a new adventure for her.

The text I would like to use is one of the Gospels that was suggested for today, John 8:1-11. I would like to focus on verses 7-11. If you would, please come with me as we reconstruct the setting and share together this great scripture.

Jesus is six months from the cross. It is early in the morning. He's at the temple and a crowd has already gathered. He is speaking to the crowd. All of a sudden, several scribes, the teachers of the law, and several Pharisees appear, dragging a woman through the crowd to where Jesus is standing.

"Teacher," they say to Jesus, *"this woman was caught in the very act of adultery. Moses' law says stone her. What do you say?"* Now they were trying to trick Jesus into saying something that could be used against him. But Jesus stooped and began to write in the dust with his finger. Now for the verses I want to focus on, verse 7 and following: They demanded again, *"What about it?"* What about the woman?"

Jesus stood up and said, *"All right, throw the stones at her until she dies! But, only he who has never sinned may throw the first stone."* As he stooped once again to write in the dust, a hush fell over the crowd, and the Jewish leaders—one by one, starting with the oldest—slipped away.

Jesus again stood up, and looking into the eyes of the woman, said to her, *"Where are your accusers? Didn't even one condemn you?"*

"No, Sir," she said. And Jesus said, *"Neither do I. Go and sin no more."*

John 8:1-11 is a very interesting scripture. Some Bible scholars are not even sure that it's in the right place. Some say it should be after John 21. Others say Luke 21, and some say it should be after John 7. I'm not concerned about whether or not it is in the right place. What I'm concerned about this morning is that it tells me once again about Jesus' love for the sinner. Jesus himself was without sin, but it seems that he loved to forgive. How his heart went out in sympathy for those who were having a hard time with their sins. This text tells me emphatically and without reservation or doubt—Jesus loves me.

Earlier I said that I was a farmer. I raise corn and soybeans. You come to church this morning to hear the Gospel preached. Instead of finding one of your pastors in the pulpit you find a farmer—and the bulletin says it is Prison Ministry Sunday. I would like for you to know why I'm here and where I'm coming from. I will try and share some of that with you as we talk about this text and Prison Ministry Sunday and how I became involved.

This scripture tells me Jesus loves the sinner—me, you, all of us—and that includes the men and the women locked up in county jails or state prisons, or federal prisons, or anywhere else. It includes the families of the prisoners, and of course, it includes the victims and those close to them. If Jesus loves me and you, all of us, that much, can that mean anything other than we should love each other? The second lesson this morning says that very thing. Remember Hebrews 13:1-3?

Several years ago I was invited to a Lutheran Retreat called Kogudus. Kogudus, I found out, was an Estonian word and meant a coming together for Christian fellowship. Studying the Creed and what it means to us, we talked about our own pilgrimage in life, and that Christ assured us, no matter where it took us, he would never leave us or forsake us. We were asked to consider what that meant to us as we went home to our families, our jobs and our churches.

That retreat had a real impact on me as I began to realize what the church meant to me. You see, it is the church that has kept the word and the sacraments alive—and it's through the church that the Gospel is preached. You and I know about Jesus Christ because someone from the church, the body of believers, told us.

The next year I noticed an article in the Kogudus national newsletter asking if there were any volunteers who would go to Montana for a

Kogudus in prison. This had never been attempted before, but the chaplain there had attended a Kogudus on the outside and thought it might work for the men in prison.

We had a young man from our community who was a member of our church living with us. He had been in prison and was supposed to go back because of a parole violation. We convinced the judge and his parole officer that he would be better off living with our family rather than going back to prison. While he was living with us, he attended a Kogudus. By this time quite a few people in our community had attended one also.

This young man, myself and two others volunteered to go to Montana. We left at three o'clock on a Wednesday morning, just before Labor Day weekend, and drove 1,600 miles to Deer Lodge, Montana, where the state prison is located. Vicki went along for prayer support and encouragement. We met several volunteers from Montana also.

It was pretty frightening. I had never been in a prison before. It was maximum security, old and outdated. The guards still walked the front wall along the street that went right through the middle of town. Vicki stayed at the motel in town and we spent the weekend in prison. We ate all our meals there and we slept in the cells. As frightening as it was, it was a great experience for us.

Before we left to go to Montana, several people in our community got together with us and held a prayer service, and also gave us six hundred prayer support letters for the residents. We had all the names of those who would be attending so the men all got a lot of personal letters. For most of them, this was more letters than they had gotten since they were in prison. They also gave us $600 for the trip. The only stipulation was that we had to take it easy on the way home and spend a little time resting and unwinding.

After the retreat, I remember all of us sitting in the grass at Yellowstone Park watching a large moose graze on the other side of a mountain stream, and I wondered, what now? Will we go to prisons in Illinois or will this be the end? A couple of years went by and the Lutheran chaplain from Menard Prison at Chester, Illinois called and said he wanted to talk to us about a thing he had heard of called Kogudus.

We scheduled one and have since gone back several times. After Menard we also went to Vandalia, Dwight, Hillsboro, Centralia, Danville, Lincoln, and Vienna. We also went to Wisconsin to a federal prison and last August, we went back to Wisconsin to Green Bay Correctional Center. This spring and early summer we have retreats planned for Lincoln, Danville, Sheridan, Menard, and Vienna.

The Kogudus program is just one of many ways to spread the good news of the Gospel, but it's been a big thing for a lot of us. It very simply is a short course in Christianity as the Lutheran Church sees it. It is kind of a refresher course on some of what we learned in confirmation with special emphasis on the church and our ministry in life. One of the things I really liked about the new Evangelical Lutheran Church of America that I heard from the beginning was that everyone is a minister, every day—everywhere. That is what Kogudus is all about.

Kogudus in prison grew out of a need. If you would attend a Kogudus you would not be expected to be involved with the prison ministry unless you wanted to. The prison part of it is kind of a mission project.

Two years ago, because of my involvement with Prison Kogudus, I was asked to become a part of the Illinois Network of Prison and Jail Ministries. Lutheran Social Services of Illinois is helping to pull that together and is responsible for some of the expense and some of the expertise. Lutheran Social Services can help you or your congregation if you are interested in prison ministry. Maybe you don't want to get that involved. If not, there are people right here in your area who are planning a retreat at Danville. You could volunteer to help with the retreat by writing letters or offering prayer support.

Is there a need for the church to be involved in prison ministry? Last year I watched a CBS special on prisons. They said, and I quote: "There are 1,000,000 people behind bars and fences in the United States." They went on to say that this will increase by 50 percent by the year 2000. U.S. prisons have doubled in the last decade. Prison population has grown five times as much as the crime rate. Most states are under court order to build new prisons. President Bush will need to spend five billion dollars on federal prisons alone.

Let's get a little closer to home. When I first went into a state prison in Illinois in the '70s, they told me there were ten thousand people incarcerated in the state of Illinois. Early last year the number has risen to twenty thousand; by October the count was 23,699, and in December it was 24,254. Last week I heard on TV it hit twenty-five thousand. This is adults-only, in-state prisons. This does not include juveniles or federal prisons or the county jails. I've never been there, but I've been told there are seven thousand people in Cook County Jail. Approximately seventy people are taken into the system every week. We are right now 33 percent over capacity. More prisons are being built, even as we are here, and more are on the drawing board. The last count I have there were twenty-one adult correctional centers in the state, five work camps, fourteen community centers, seven youth centers, two federal prisons, and all the county jails besides that.

Depending on the prison, it costs between $16,000 and $20,000 to keep a person in a prison for one year. It's cheaper to send a man to Harvard than it is to send a man to prison. Just last week I read what I felt was a rather startling fact. There are over fifteen thousand people incarcerated in state prisons in the Central Southern Illinois Synod of the ELCA. Your church and my church are in the Central Southern Illinois Synod.

What about the children and the families of those in prison? Lutheran Social Services tells us there are children in downstate

Illinois who do not get to visit their father or mother in prison with any regularity because there is no one to take them. What about the children? Maybe some of you would like to help the children. Maybe you could take them.

This week while I was thinking about the Gospel text for today, I thought, what if I was dragged through a crowd to where Jesus stood, and my accusers who held me laid my sins out for Jesus and the whole crowd to see and hear? How ashamed and panic stricken I would be. But then, as my eyes met the eyes of a forgiving Savior, I would hear him say, *"I do not condemn you. Go—and care for those I have placed around you. Be compassionate to them, as I am to you, and reach out in forgiveness and understanding."*

I can't help but think of the thousands who have been placed right here in our synod. They, too, have been dragged before the crowds—only to be found guilty. Instead of being told to go and sin no more, they've been told, "At this time you can no longer live and move in society." For the most part there is nothing we can do about that—or maybe should do about that; but many do not know the forgiveness of the Savior. And those who do know Christ need to be encouraged and supported in their struggle to bring some meaning to their life.

"What good do you do?" I'm often asked. "How many lives are really changed? How successful are you?" Are lives changed? Sure, sometimes, but we can't change lives. Only God can do that. Nor can we take the blame if lives are not changed. Are we successful? The success is that we get to go and tell the story, and no one can ever be the same after hearing the Gospel.

What about those you find in prison? What are they like? They are a lot like you and me. Maybe more lonely, maybe more frustrated, sometimes more angry. Many have taken a wrong turn by a series of mistakes amplified by a poor environment, or poor family ties, or from being a minority. Maybe drugs or alcohol are a problem. I remember once we were in the middle of a retreat on Saturday morning, getting ready to go to lunch. I said, "Let's say the Lord's Prayer and break for lunch." As we bowed our heads to pray, I remember this young man, maybe eighteen years old, standing beside me. He reached over and touched my arm. "I don't know what the Lord's Prayer is," he said. That night back at the hotel I remember thinking, "What would I be like if I never had heard of the Lord's Prayer until I was eighteen?"

In our text for today, Jesus was six months from the cross. On the last day of this month it will be Ash Wednesday—the beginning of Lent. We, too, are just a short time from the Cross of Easter. This cross brought forgiveness to us and to the church. How can we not be involved? As Lent approaches, let us consider what Jesus wants the church to do about prison ministry. Amen.

27

"Ministry in Daily Life"

St. John's Lutheran Church, Bloomington, IL

Lutheran Men in Mission—NE Conference

September 15, 1990

Good afternoon. My name is Jerry Crane. I'm a layman from Hartsburg, Illinois, and I go to church at St. Peter's Lutheran in Emden where Reverend Frank Pieper is pastor. I'm here to visit with you for a few minutes about Kogudus. "Kogudus" means a gathering—a coming together in a retreat-type setting.

Kogudus is a lay-ministry movement under the guidance of the pastor, calling for the renewal of commitment to Christ, to his church and to his call to serve, and to the affirmation of the ministry of all God's people. Our bishop says our ministry begins with personal renewal. Our prayer at Kogudus is *"Come, Holy Spirit. Revive your church. Begin with me."*

So why a presentation on Kogudus here at your convention today? Is all this renewal stuff necessary? Do we have to talk of commitment and go to retreats? The president of Pacific Lutheran Theological Seminary in Berkley, California, states it this way: "We Christians have a lot of power stored up like dynamite waiting to go off! Whether or not it will ever go off is up to us. I know this," he goes on to say, "if we could ever get the stuff lit, the power released would rearrange our congregations, our ministries, and our priorities in life." This power—this dynamite he is talking about—is ministry in daily life.

Ministry in daily life. We are hearing that more and more since the formation of the new church. What is my ministry in life? I'm a layperson; most of you are. Do we have a calling? What about where I work or where I play—or when I'm with my family? Is there a need there? Of course there is, and if there is a need there, we know Jesus is saying, *"Take heart, I am there and I want you there."*

On August 26 on the back of our church bulletin, a paragraph caught my eye. It said, "If you think you have no calling—or your calling has lost direction—listen once more. *You are where you are so that Christ can be there."* That, my friends, is what I believe our ministry in daily life is. *We are where we are so that Christ can be there.*

How can the LMM in your Northeast Conference be involved with the Kogudus renewal ministry? Let me tell you how our neighbors to the south in the Arkansas-Oklahoma Synod are doing it. Several of us will be traveling to Tulsa, Oklahoma, to help them with their first Kogudus on November 16, 17, and 18. I've told you what the president of a seminary said. I've read a letter of recommendation from the president of LMM. Maybe I should share with you what I feel about Kogudus.

It was at Kogudus that I discovered what the church had been teaching me all along. I came away with a new love for the church and for its people. You see, the church is where it's at. It's the church that's kept the word and the sacraments alive, and it's the church that Christ has used to keep his people together. I know about Christ because someone from the church told me.

What is our ministry in life? Yes, it's going to take commitment and it's going to take renewal. Kogudus can provide a setting to help us consider these essential priorities in life. Thank you very much for allowing me time to be here.

28

"We Are Where We Are so Christ Can Be There"

Macon, MO—

December 9, 1990

Good morning! As Dick Hilgendorf and your bulletin said, my name is Jerry Crane and I'm a farmer from Hartsburg, Illinois. Hartsburg is a town of about 350 people and is located about halfway between Peoria and Springfield, Illinois. I'm glad to be with you here in Macon.

In the late '70s I made trips to Macon on a regular basis because Dick and I had bought some land together. I later sold my part and haven't had occasion to be back since then. I always thought Macon was a great place with a lot of good people. Once when my family was out here over a weekend, we went to church in your former building.

Now if I were you, and I was sitting out there looking at me standing in your pulpit, I would wonder, "What's so special about him that he would drive out here from Illinois to speak to us this morning?"

Let me assure you that I'm just an ordinary farmer with an ordinary education who's made a lot of ordinary mistakes. The only thing that is extraordinary about me is my wife, who is with me this morning.

I talked to Dick Friday evening and he told me it said in the bulletin that I would be talking this morning about retreats. I'll just touch on that a little. I've been involved with a Lutheran retreat called Kogudus. "Kogudus" means a coming together for Christian fellowship. It's kind of a short course in Christianity and has been very meaningful to me. A lot of people in our community have been involved, as Dick also has, and it has really helped us to appreciate what the Church has been telling us all along.

There have been Kogudus retreats in many parts of the U.S. and some of us have traveled to Texas, Florida, Minnesota, Wisconsin, Hawaii, California, Montana, and Arizona. During this past year, several of us from our area went to western Kansas, and just a couple of weeks ago we went to Tulsa, Oklahoma, to help them get started with Kogudus. Kogudus has also been to Canada, Germany, and Australia. We've also been to over a dozen state and federal prisons in Montana, Illinois, and Wisconsin.

Kogudus not only helps us to think about the basic things that are really important, it also helps us to realize that we lay people, too, have a ministry in life. It's not just the pastor who has a ministry. We all do.

A few weeks ago I read one of the greatest things I think I've ever read concerning lay people—people like you and me. It said, "I am where I am so Christ can be there." Isn't that something? We may be just a farmer, or a factory worker, or a businessman, or a housewife, or a student, but we are where we are so Christ can be there. We lay people have a job to do. The pastor can't do it all. "I don't know enough," you say. "I can't quote the scriptures, or say great, meaningful things." I found out a long time ago that people really don't care how much you know if they know how much you care.

We are living in a great world, but this world is full of heartache and sickness, tragedy and loneliness, and people need the comfort that only Christ can give them. Most of the time, the comfort of Christ comes through people like you and me. We all know people who are hurting, and most of us have been there ourselves. Some of us may be there right now and need someone.

If you would like to know more about Kogudus, ask Dick. He'll be glad to tell you about it, and better yet, maybe you could get a carload of men together to come to Illinois for a men's retreat in January. It would be great to have you there!

So much for retreats. I'd like to visit with you this morning concerning the second lesson that Dick just read: II Peter 3:2. I'd like to start at verse 10 (RSV): *"But the day of the Lord will come like a thief, and then the heavens will pass away with a loud noise, and the elements will be dissolved with fire, and the earth and the works that are upon it will be burned up . . . But according to his promise we wait for new heavens and a new earth in which righteousness dwells."* That's kind of scary, isn't it? To think that the world would be destroyed, or at least burnt up, and made new.

There's been a lot of talk lately about the earthquake and the New Madrid fault. They say there is really a good chance that there will be a major earthquake in parts of Missouri and Illinois in the next few years. It's frightening to think about something happening to the earth. The earth is supposed to be so secure. But God's purpose for mankind is not destruction—it's re-creation. The lesson this morning tells us he will purify the earth and heavens and make them new.

How will this happen? I don't know. Jesus said no one knows the day or the hour, but it will come like a thief in the night. We must be ready. This scripture brings back a lot of memories for me. Several years ago our son Tim died after developing complications from injuries suffered in a van accident. At that moment, nothing was important except Tim's relationship with his Lord.

The next morning after Tim died, Vicki and I were lying in bed talking and Vicki said it was just like a thief in the night. We thought he was going to be okay, but death came, like a thief in the night. Why do I tell you this? This story is not any greater or any less than your story. I'm not the only one who has lost a son or someone very close to them. I share this story with you because it is the story God shared with me through our son and his death.

If you lost someone close to you and you were not able to be with him or her before he or she died, please know it's still okay. God is fair and loving and just even though things are different than we would have planned them. He loves us all.

I guess through this scripture this morning, and I hope through this story I just shared with you, God is saying to all of us, *"My dear chosen people, if you are not ready, it's time to get ready, for we know not the day or the hour, and very soon, whether it be at the end of our life or the end of the world as we know it, we'll be coming home to God where there is no more pain, or loneliness, or sickness, or tragedy, when we will see our loved ones again, and finally, finally spend eternity with peace and joy."*

Good people here in Macon, it will soon be Christmas, the day we celebrate Christ's birthday. We need to share that Christmas—and Easter—message with those around us. There are still many who do not know, and there are many who know, who need support and comfort. Remember, even though we are just lay people, we have a ministry. We are where we are so Christ can be there.

God bless you all. Have a great Christmas and thanks for letting me and Vicki worship with you this morning. Amen.

29

"God's Grace for All"

Presbyterian Church

Criminal Justice Week

1987

Father, we thank you for this morning that you have given us. As we gather here together to worship you, help us to be unified in you. We thank you for the gift of your grace. We pray for Reverend Schwartz and his family and for this congregation. May they continue to hear your word and may they understand your will.

On this Sunday of Criminal Justice Week, we pray for men and women incarcerated in prison. We pray for their families. We pray for the victims who are too numerous to number.

Lord Jesus, we pray for those in law enforcement: policemen, judges, those serving on juries. Give them your wisdom. We pray for wardens and guards. We pray for prison chaplains as they bring your word to lonely hearts.

We ask that your healing hand be with those, especially in this congregation, who are sick or hurting or grieving. You know, Lord, who they are.

Please bless the service this morning that it may honor you. We ask these things in Jesus' name, who taught us to pray (The Lord's Prayer). Amen.

The second reading this morning is from Paul's letter to the Ephesians, chapter 1:4-8 and 2:1-7.

Good morning. I'm glad to be here to worship with you this morning. The theme for today is "God's Grace for All." But, if I were you and came to church this morning and saw this farmer standing in the pulpit and had heard that he attends a Lutheran Church, I might say, "What's happening here?"

Well, as John said, my name is Jerry Crane, and I do farm near Hartsburg. Hartsburg is located about halfway between Peoria and Springfield on Route 121. If you've ever driven from Morton south to Lincoln, you've gone right by our home. I farm with my son, Todd, and last year, my son-in-law Benjie, who is with me this morning and has started to help us.

I was here last November for your couples' group, "The Mariners," when our friends, Buzz and Kay Davis, invited us.

I was brought up in a very small Presbyterian country church, and it was there that I attended Sunday school and later was confirmed. The doors of that church closed about the time Vicki and I were married, so I transferred my membership to St. Peter's Lutheran in Emden, where we are members today.

I have some great memories of that little Presbyterian Church. During high school, I was the janitor, and I fired the coal furnace. I'd have to start really early when it was cold, so the church would be warm for Sunday school, and I can remember sitting in that cold church all by myself, waiting for the fire to take hold, and wondering about "the mysteries of God."

The book of Ephesians was chosen for the second reading this morning. I understand that Ephesians is one of the four "prison letters" that Paul wrote when he himself was incarcerated in Rome. You know, that's kind of amazing that a man in prison the biggest part of two thousand years ago could write a letter and that you and I would be reading it today.

It seems as though Paul was telling those people in Ephesus, and those of us gathered here this morning, one of the greatest revelations of truth that God has given his people. The King James Version of the Bible implies that what Paul is saying here explains a mystery that had been hidden since before the foundation of the world. In other words, it must have been in the heart of God even before the beginning.

How can we know about this mystery? It can be known to us only if God chooses to reveal it to us, and he has through Paul in his letter we read this morning. What does this have to do with Criminal Justice Week? I believe a lot! It might even be the reason for having it.

Paul is talking about the "Grace of God for all." He was talking to Jews and Gentiles, people with completely different lifestyles and beliefs. Yet he was saying it for all! For Paul, Christ was a great big Savior, something so big that there was room for people who have different values, viewpoints, and yes, even prejudices, and that he had, and still has, the power to bring unity to all people.

Christ has the power to unify people, even with all their differences and misconceptions. How? Through the mystery of his *extraordinary grace*. Everyone needs it. Everyone must have it. And no matter what differences we have, we come together to receive the same thing—God's grace.

Fourteen years ago in 1973, I was invited to attend a Christian retreat called Kogudus. I didn't have the foggiest idea what it was, let alone what the word Kogudus meant. It started on a Friday evening with a steak dinner and ended Sunday afternoon after church. About twenty-five to thirty men gathered at a fraternity house in Urbana over semester break, and we stayed there for the whole weekend. We talked about listening to God and listening to those around us. We talked about the Apostles' Creed and about our own statement of faith. Before we left, we were challenged to think about God's plan for our lives.

I guess it doesn't sound like much, but it was a big deal for me. I left that retreat with a new appreciation for God's gift of grace to me, and a new appreciation for the church. I had no idea I owed the church, God's body of believers down through the years, so much. I knew I needed God's grace, and the church was what had kept this message alive so I could hear it and know it was there. The church, with all its differences, all its shortcomings and all its prejudices, even with all these things going against it, God's people still united with Christ to preserve the message so all of us could hear it. Isn't that something?

"Kogudus" by the way, I found out, was an Estonian word and meant Christian fellowship. The reason it was called Kogudus was because the pastor who started the retreat, Pastor Magis, was from Estonia and, in fun, wanted to get something in the retreat from his background, and the name Kogudus stuck.

I also learned that his father was a pastor in Estonia, and while Pastor Magis was studying for the ministry, war broke out in Estonia. They found themselves in the middle of the Nazi and communist conflict, and as he fled, he was captured and put into prison. Later, after escaping, he was placed in a displaced persons' camp. The church from America reached out and brought him and other refugees to America. He was able to finish his schooling here and become a pastor. That was one of the reasons why the love for the church came out so much at Kogudus.

The next year, we received a newsletter from the Kogudus national office in Montana. It seemed that a pastor from Montana who happened to be a prison chaplain had attended a Kogudus and wanted to try one for men in prison. It was to be an experiment, and they wanted some volunteers for a team. Pastor Magis wasn't anxious to go. He remembered all too well his own prison experience years ago as he left his homeland.

Vicki and I had a young man living with us who earlier had robbed a doctor's office and had spent a year in Vandalia Correctional Center. After he was paroled, he was in a small auto accident and drugs were found in the car. This automatically violated his parole, and he was to go back to prison. Vicki and I talked to him and his parole officer, and then went to court, and somehow the judge was persuaded to let him live with us rather than go back to prison.

While he was living with us, he went to Kogudus, and this put new meaning in his life. He volunteered to go to Montana. Two other young men who we knew really well had gone to Kogudus, and they wanted to go too. I suppose I'm making Kogudus sound like a cure-all for wayward people. It isn't. It just happened that it was an important event in all their lives.

One night on July 4, they were all at our house, and everyone was excited about going out of state for the first prison Kogudus. I didn't know; it was a big step. It would take a couple of months for the prison chaplain to clear it with his administration. It was already July 4. Two months would put us close to harvest, and we had a thousand acres of crops to get in. One of the guys was going back to the University of Illinois that fall, and school would already be started. Another had a job and would have to take time off. Someone suggested we pray about it.

We did . . . and we went on Labor Day weekend, 1,600 miles to Deer Lodge, Montana—four of us and Vicki, who stayed in a motel down the street from the prison and was our prayer partner. Others in our community who had attended Kogudus retreats met and sent six hundred prayer support letters for us and the inmates and $600 for our expenses. A lot of things came from that Montana retreat. More stories than we could get into this morning, including an Indian who came and lived with us for over a year. But those stories aren't so important for what we are talking about this morning.

Paul, in his letter to the Ephesians, was talking about unity—unity through Christ. While the prison retreat was going on, I had unity with the men in prison. After all, we were all sinners, and it was a great experience. But after the retreat, I thought about my own life, and I remember talking to a prison chaplain from Illinois who shared my thoughts, although I hadn't told him. He said, "I'm not like some of those men. I haven't killed or raped or stolen someone's money and that's good. We shouldn't do anything that harms others or harms society." I felt the same way. But then I thought, Jesus, the one handing out the grace says in Matthew 5, *"You have heard the men of old say, 'Do not kill for whosoever kills is in danger of judgment,' but I say unto you that whoever is angry with his brother without a cause shall be in danger of judgment."*

"You have heard that it says, 'Do not commit adultery,' but I say anyone who even looks at another with lust in their heart has already committed adultery. Thou shalt not covet your neighbor's . . ." Sometimes there is a

fine line between stealing and our ways in the business world as we add to our own possessions, taking something that is really our neighbor's possession or our neighbor's job or one of our neighbor's accounts. Yes, I am one of those Paul is addressing his letter to. I have a different lifestyle, a different view. Yes, I do have prejudices that differ from others. I have prejudices I don't even know about, but through Christ there is room for me.

We have had over twenty prison Kogudus retreats in Illinois alone, and this spring and early summer we have four more scheduled and are working with two others. There was a time when I wanted the men and myself who came to prison on the Kogudus team, and the residents on the inside, to be one. It probably will happen that we can be one only in Christ. We have different views and lifestyles and prejudices. We are different. All of God's people are different. But that, my friends, is the miracle. *God's grace is for all!*

Several years ago, I was going through one of the hardest times I could imagine. My fourteen-year-old son had died eleven days after a van accident. I remember, and want to share with you, the content of one of the many letters I received. It was from an inmate. He said to me, and I quote, "May God let me die before you, and may God grant me, no matter in what far corner of heaven I might be, that on the day you die, he will bring me to that place where you and your son shall meet again, so that I can share in your happiness." I do not know where that resident is today. We were different, but for a moment, he shared with me the love of Christ, and we were one in our mourning. Yes, he and I were different, but together, we can share the love of Christ with the rest of the world.

You see, everyone needs God's grace. I have to have it. The inmates have to have it. The victims have to have it. The warden has to have it, the guards, the judges, the jury, the policemen, Billy Graham, the Pope, Reverend Schwartz, Buzz Davis. We are all different, but in Christ there's room, and we come together to receive his grace. He has already given it. *God's grace is for all!* All we have to do is accept it.

Footnote: Wendelin Black died as a result of a car accident shortly after being released from prison. Jerry received a letter from the prison chaplain that read, "After your many prayers and special efforts on his behalf, I know the news of his death will also grieve you. I only wish that he'd been able to follow through on his dreams and talk of seeing you people after he was released. But, it was not to be."

Part IV

School and Community Events

30. "May Your Dreams Come True"—Hartem High School Graduation, 1979 181
31. "Man on the Road"—Logan County Fair," 1989 189
32. "Revisiting My Childhood"—Hartsburg Fireman's Day, 1990 193
33. "The Gift of Compassion"—Browning Junior High Athletic Banquet, 1993 197
34. "Suffering Is Not Wasted"—Memorial Day Service, Hartsburg Cemetery, 1993 203

30

"May Your Dreams Come True"

Hartsburg-Emden High School Graduation

May, 1979

I was trying to figure out an opening line tonight, so I thought back to how most professional speakers who speak here at the school start out. They usually say something like, "It certainly is a pleasure to be here in Hartsburg tonight speaking to you fine people in this agriculture community." I was born and raised on a farm myself, but that opening somehow doesn't seem too impressive. Most of you kind of know that already, so, so much for the opening line.

But it is a pleasure—more than a pleasure—it's exciting to be here tonight. Exciting, because it makes me feel really good to be able to visit with this class a little while. This happens to be a very special class to me. Some of you people were at our house for a first-grade birthday party. I've known some of you a long time—all your life. I saw Rick

Hanna when he was a couple of hours old. I thought I was going to see Amy, but her mom decided to wait a couple of more days.

I've been able to sit back and watch you. I've seen you happy and sad, good and bad. There's a lot of talent in this class, as there is in every other class, a lot of leadership ability, good athletes, good workers, those with musical ability and there will be some scholars and very learned people that will come forward from this class. There's a lot of things that I've found out over the years about you people—about your talents and abilities.

Last fall there was a wiener roast and hayrack ride at our house for this class. I was really surprised at some of the many talents and abilities this class has produced. For instance, did you know that when this class goes on a hayrack ride, you don't need a hayrack? They all run along the side—sure, the girls too. Most of these people can run ten to fifteen miles at a stretch. Lisa James can run full speed across town with a bale of straw on her shoulder. Beats anything I ever did see. Lori Eeten, she's the fastest, at least that night. She could leave everyone else in the dust anytime she wanted to.

But the real talent I believe this class has, is in their corn-shucking ability. You know how you've all heard those old farmers talk about how much corn they could shuck by hand in a day? Like Mr. Polly, for instance, he used to always tell me how much corn he could shuck in a day. Did he ever tell you that? But this class—you've never seen anything like it. They can run ahead of the hayrack, jump out in a field, shuck twenty or thirty bushels of corn in a matter of seconds, throw it on the rack wagon and then run on. Once we stopped the tractor to wait on some people who were about a mile back down the road—we had kids scattered over about a four-mile area, and the rest of the class shucked about ten acres of Trojan corn for Melvin Fink. If any of these people decide to farm, they'll never need a combine.

Seriously, this is a great class. Quite honestly, it's a class that makes some people a little nervous. You never know quite what to expect next. But let me say this—that's not all bad. Though they don't always show it (sometimes you have to look close), there are some real thinkers in this class. Some people may say dreamers, that's the word I'm looking for. That's the word I hope I can see when I look at this class—people who can dream—and make that dream become a reality. To be able to dream and say, "That's what I want, that's what I want for my life." And after dreaming and planning be able to say, "Not only what I want, but what God wants for me. It's what he wants me to be—what he wants me to do."

Dreams are not a waste of time. Dreams are not something we do because we are lazy or wish we could be away from where we are. Dreams are developed in our minds—minds that are part of a living, breathing, functioning body—which are created by a living, breathing, functioning God. So many times we put down those who dream. They're way out there in left field, we say, trying to escape reality, but that isn't necessarily so. In fact, every good thing that was ever completed started with a dream. A dream that at one time (usually the day after it was first thought of) seemed like one of the craziest ideas you ever heard of. That would be too much work, take too much time, you say. But it keeps working on you and you share it with someone else, someone you think you can depend on, and even they say it's crazy, it won't work, you aren't capable of doing that. But let me say this: God will never give you a job that you can't do. He knows what you are capable of and he won't let you down.

A couple of years ago I became acquainted with one of the most dynamic men I have ever met, a man who started with a dream while he was locked in prison in a displaced persons' camp during the war. Last month we flew to Texas together and while en route, he said,

"Jerry, those dreams—don't shove them back. Think about them, pray about them, no matter how silly or preposterous they may seem. They are created in your mind, in a part of you that is so complex that only God himself can understand it, because he created it. And though many thoughts are our own—many, and yes, I believe most of our thoughts are inspired by God to help us to be and do what he wants us to do, and if he's behind them, nothing—no, nothing is impossible."

I'll help you move a mountain, he says. I will let you be anything I want you to be if only you will say okay. Okay, God. He says, I will make you a leader or will help you be a follower, and as the psalmist says in Psalm 32: "*I will instruct you, says the Lord, and guide you along the best pathway for your life. I will advise you and watch your progress.*" He's talking about your life—what you're going to be doing, where you're going in your life—that dream. He will help us make it happen. Remember that dream that was born in your mind, that mind that's part of a living, breathing, functioning body created by a living, breathing, functioning God.

Several years ago there was a song called, "My Best to You." The words went something like this: "*My best to you, may your dreams come true; may old Father Time never be unkind. And through the years, save your smiles and tears; they are souvenirs—they'll make music in your heart. Remember this, each new day's a kiss, sent from up above with God's heavenly love. So here's to you, may your dreams come true, and your love blessed, that's my best to you.*"

May your dreams come true. And you know what's so great about dreams? Anybody can do it. They don't have to be a big thing that happens, that throws you into a trance, or knocks you to the ground. It doesn't have to happen while seeing or being with someone great. Dreams just come usually as a passing thought, a thought that just won't leave you alone. Let me give you a couple of examples. It would be easy to talk about dreams like Alexander Graham Bell had, that people someday might communicate many miles apart, or John Kennedy, who dreamed of the presidency. Let's look closer at people we know and see.

Several years ago, I was a member of this school board here. One of the first things I was involved with was to help hire a principal. After looking over several applications, we decided to interview a man who had left the field of education for a while, but had decided to come back. An interview was set up and he arrived that night right on time, but he looked worn out from what must have been a long day. In fact, he looked almost like he needed a shave. I felt right away that he surely wasn't the man for the job. Sometime after the interview started, it became apparent that his day had been a long one and he was running late, but rather than cancel the interview or be late, he came as he was, and it also became apparent that he was interested in the job.

As the possibility of him being the next principal at the school was discussed, you could see a new look on his face and in his eyes, and I knew then he would get my vote. I couldn't quite put my finger on it, but behind those eyes—in that mind, yes, once again a mind that's part of a living, breathing, functioning body created by a living, breathing, functioning God was a dream. But it wasn't until sometime later that I knew what that dream was. It was not to be just principal, but I think, superintendent of a school district—this school district. This dream kept him here at Hartsburg-Emden as principal for three years, and then this dream took him many miles away to southern Illinois—yet not to be fulfilled there either.

Then it happened. The superintendent here at Hartsburg-Emden left and he was called back, called back and asked to be superintendent here. He's sitting on this stage right now. You all know who I'm talking about—Roger Ingle. A dream that was started years ago. One that wouldn't be particularly easy even after it was in the process of becoming a reality. Like the song says: *"your smiles and tears, they are souvenirs."* Those problems, those tears, they are what make it worthwhile, to know that you let the dream, no matter how hard it was, you let it become a reality. God's good time always lets them happen if we are willing to say okay—okay.

Where will Roger's next dream lead him? To somewhere else or to make this school district *more*—and *better*? I, of course, don't know. I don't know if Roger knows either. But it was a dream and it happened.

I want to give you one more example. A couple I've known for several years, a couple who, these past few years, I've grown to know and love, decided they wanted more from life. They wanted a child, and not having any, decided to adopt one. Now adoption can be a long, slow process and there is always the anxiety of "Will the baby fit into our family, our relationship? Will he or she be good? How will he turn out?" It's so much trouble, so much waiting. You have to lay yourself out to caseworkers, throw open the doors to your home. It really doesn't seem worth it. It's just a dream. Let's just put it in the back of our minds. It's too much trouble. It, no doubt, will be expensive. Without the baby we can both work, both be free, and not be tied down. But that dream hangs in there so you pursue it. And three years later, a simple phone call and the person on the other end of the phone says, "You can pick up your new baby boy next week."

Was it worth it? What about the trouble he will cause? What about those nights when he is sick and you walk the floor with him? What about those near accidents that almost happen to every child and the nights you stay up worrying about him as he becomes older? Is it worth it? Was that three-year-old dream worth it? You be the judge. You tell me if it was worth it. Duane, bring Jason up here, will you?

You bet it's worth it, because it was a dream—a dream born (here it comes again) in a mind that's part of a living, breathing, functioning body created by a living, breathing, functioning God. And because of this dream, all our lives are a little different, because you can't bring a person into this small community without him touching many people—maybe every one of us—in some small, or not-so-small way, and because of their dream, our lives may be different.

Well, just a couple examples of dreams of people you know. People who had a dream and let those dreams come true. I hope Barb, Duane, and Mr. Ingle didn't mind me sharing those thoughts with you. We all dream, but we let so many of our dreams die away—good dreams—gone by the wayside, because they're too much trouble, because we don't have time to wait—many reasons.

You know God himself had a dream once. And in his dream, he thought, *"I'm alone. I'll create—I'll create the heavens and the earth and I'll make man and I'll bless him,"* and he did. He formed man from the dust and breathed into him the breath of life, and man became a living person. And it was God's dream that man become one with him, but man chose to go against God, and because of God's love he said okay; and man ruined God's dream, or it appeared that he did. But God said, *"No, I will not give up my dream. My dream will come true and man shall come and live with me forever—those that want to."* So God came to earth in the form of a man. Jesus was his name. And God's dream came true, but it wasn't easy. In fact, he had to go the way of the cross so that his dream could come true. Was it worth it, just to let a dream come true? God says it was, because in Hebrews 12:2, it says that he himself endured the cross because of the joy, because of the joy he knew would follow, that if he said okay to his dream, okay to the cross, man could be reunited with him. Yes, no matter what it takes, even a cross, it's worth it to let your dreams come true.

And now, if I may speak to all of you for just a moment about dreams—these young people's dreams. We all want them to dream dreams and be all that God wants them to be. But do we—do we really? Are we willing to sacrifice ourselves for them? Give them some of our time, and some of our prayers to help their dreams come true? Each one of us has a very important paper in our hands. It looks like a program and it is, but it's more than that, because it has the name of everyone in the class in it. We have in our possession a ready-made prayer list.

How many people are here tonight? Two hundred or two hundred and fifty? If we really care about these people and their dreams, not one of us should go to bed tonight without going over this list in prayer and asking God to bless each one of these graduates. Bless each one with the dreams that God has in mind for them. Imagine two hundred and fifty prayers for each one of these young people tonight!

So in your dreams remember this: *Each new day's a kiss sent from up above with God's heavenly love. So here's to you. May your dreams come true, and your love blessed—that's my best to you.*

31

"Man on the Road"

Logan County Fair, Lincoln, IL

August 6, 1989

We're glad to see you here this morning. If you're thinking, "I don't know what to expect here," I want to assure you, you're not alone. I don't believe any of us quite do. It will be a very informal service. We will have a couple of songs, a prayer, scripture reading, some special music, a short message, and a closing, probably lasting somewhere around an hour.

I must admit that as long as I've been coming to the fair, I personally have never been involved in a worship service. I've done a lot of other things, especially about thirty-five years ago down at the 4-H barns, but that was a long way from what we are about this morning.

It seems to be another great fair, and as it comes to a close, like a lot of other things in this great country, we have a lot to be thankful for—from the young people in 4-H being able to show the fruits of their labor, to being entertained, to remembering all those who worked so hard to make it happen, and last, and certainly not least, to a God who, for some reason, has blessed us to be a part of what Logan County is all about.

The text for this morning will be from the lesson that Dean Bruns read from Hebrews, in particular Hebrews 11:1-3. It went something like this: *"Now faith is the assurance of things hoped for, the conviction of things not seen. For by it [this faith] men of old [like Moses, Abraham, and other prophets] received divine approval. By faith we understand that the world was created by the word of God, so that what is seen was made out of things which were not seen."*

I want to share some thoughts I have about the first lesson that Dean read. By sharing thoughts with you, it's okay to agree or disagree, because thoughts and feelings are just that—thoughts and feelings. They are neither right nor wrong—they just are.

Hebrews 11 is the great chapter of the illustration of faith. The question of faith has, no doubt, come up in all our minds at some time or another. A little boy, when asked what faith is, said, after much thought, "Faith is believing in something you just know ain't so."

We have faith that somewhere, somehow, a great and wonderful God created the earth and sustains it. We have faith that he will continue to do that as long as he sees fit. We, as Christian people, have faith that God came to earth in a man called Jesus, so that he could die for sins that were not his, but *ours!*

We have a great need and a great desire for faith. Faith is where hope comes from. Remember Dean said faith is the assurance of things hoped for. We all have things we hope for. Have you ever met a person who has lost all hope? I met a man on the road just a couple of weeks ago. He had just gotten out of prison and had lost all hope. What I did for him was not a great thing, but what was great about it was that this time *I recognized an opportunity that God had put before me.* So many times we miss those opportunities.

Sometimes we say, "I have no faith—I can't believe it." Yet we constantly place faith in people around us. Suppose we want to go to Florida. We buy a ticket and get on a plane. Without seeing or knowing a single thing about the pilot's ability, we sit there trusting him to lift us off the ground and to gently put us down in Florida. We trust our total earthly life to him. Faith is simply trusting God and believing him. There is nothing mysterious about faith. It is a simple act. And you know what? Faith can make those of us who are weak strong.

Who is this God who wants our faith and hope and our trust? Who is this Jesus who gives us the promise of a new life and hope of eternity? It's been a long time since he walked the earth, but his presence is still with us. We have that faith and that hope.

Let's pray together: Dear Lord, we thank you that we can be here this morning, remembering you, knowing who we have faith in. We thank you for each other. We thank you for this fair. Help it to be wholesome and good for us. Please bless your people as they meet in churches everywhere this morning. Thank you especially for the young people who took part this past week with the showing and exhibits. Please bless their efforts. Bless those who worked so hard to make this all possible. Thank you, Lord, that for some reason you have blessed us to live in a place where all this takes place. Help our blessings to be a blessing for others. Lord, we remember those who are less fortunate. We remember those who travel. Grant us healing and safety. In your name we pray. Amen. Let's pray together the Lord's Prayer.

32

"Revisiting My Childhood"

Fireman's Day Hartsburg, IL

June 16, 1990

———∽∾∘⚬⟨∘⟩⚬∘∾∽———

Gayla Wibben called the other night and said they wanted a storyteller for Fireman's Day, and I said, "What do you mean a storyteller?"

She said, "Someone to tell a story."

"I can't do that," I told her.

"Sure you can," she said. "Alexis went down to the elevator and asked the guys there if they knew anyone who could tell a story and Jeff said Jerry Crane's the biggest storyteller he knew." So Jeff, thanks a lot. What in the world can I talk about? Gayla said I had five minutes. Well, when I think of Fireman's Day, I think of Founder's Day, and homecomings, and when I was a kid growing up.

Now I had the greatest time growing up any kid could ever ask for. There was so much to see and so much to do. There was work to be done and fun to be had. But one of the greatest things, when you were a freshman or sophomore in high school, was driving around on Sunday afternoon. Now I spent a lot of time on Sunday afternoons with Carl Hobbs. He had a '39 Chevy pickup he had bought from Leo Mammen—and it was cool! That truck did have one disadvantage though: about half the time, it had no brakes. Now I don't mean poor brakes. I mean pedal-to-the-floor, get-ready-to-jump no brakes!

Well, one Sunday afternoon while Carl and I were driving around with a couple of girls, we decided to drive through Hartsburg on the way home. As we came by the high school, we noticed a big crowd of people at the ball diamond—Sunday afternoon baseball. You remember those Sunday afternoon baseball games. Well, we had taken the muffler off of the truck earlier in the afternoon and this was our chance to show everyone at the ballgame just how cool we were.

Carl pressed the accelerator to the floor and as we roared by the ball diamond you could just feel how the people envied us. There was one problem: Moon Mullins. You remember Harold "Moon" Mullins, Kay's husband, a really nice, easy-going guy. Now Harold was leaving the ballgame, pulling out on the street just as we came by. He was on his side of the street okay, but we were too, and "*bang!*" we hit.

Now a '39 Chevy pickup, you remember, had big front fenders, and they curved over the wheel and down to the running board and then back to the rear fender. Now when we hit, that front fender ripped off along with the running board and was held on only by the back fender, but the whole side of the truck was at a forty-five-degree angle with the front fender about eight feet to the left of where it should be. Carl slammed on the brakes, and like I mentioned earlier, we had none. We coasted all the way to the cemetery road.

Well, we turned around and looked, and everyone was running out in the road to see if Harold was okay. We had to go back, so we turned around, and with that left side of the pickup hanging clear out in the road, drove back to the ball diamond. Harold was okay, and after we took care of the insurance stuff, we pulled the side of the pickup the rest of the way off and threw it in the back of the truck.

Now this was going to be a problem for us, because, you see, Irvin Hobbs—that's Carl's dad—you remember, had a brand-new '55 Studebaker. Now that was a machine. It was aerodynamic. It had a sloping hood and a sloping trunk and a big V8 engine, and it would go like the wind—and Carl and I were supposed to use the car that night. Now bringing that pickup home with one side off of it could spell the end of the Studebaker for us, but Carl had a plan. "Why don't you come home with me?" he said. "My folks won't get as mad if you're there."

"I don't know," I said.

"Yeah," Carl said. "It's our only chance."

Well, we went to Carl's house and his folks must have been looking out the window, because no more had we stopped in the lane and they were out there. Now Carl's mom got pretty excited, crying and carrying on, and wanted to know who we hit, and she mentioned something about a lawsuit. Well, after she finished up and went into the house, Carl and I were just standing there by the truck with our hands in our pockets and Irvin looking at us. Now Irvin didn't swear much—just when he had to make a point, but he said—well, I can't tell you exactly what he said. "Blankity-blank it, Carl, why can't you be more careful?" and he turned and went into the house.

Carl said, "That wasn't too bad. We still might have a chance at the Studebaker."

Carl had another plan. "I know Mom's frying chicken for supper," he said. "About halfway through supper, when Dad's in a good mood, you ask him for the car tonight."

"I can't do that," I said.

"You have to," Carl said. "It's our only chance." I thought I was going to be sick.

Well, surprisingly enough, supper didn't go too bad and about halfway through, I looked over at Carl and he nodded and whispered "Now!"

No one had yet said a word at supper. I broke the silence. "Boy, Irvin," I said. "You sure got that new Studebaker all shined up."

"Yep," he responded.

I looked at Carl. He nodded, go ahead. I broke the silence again, "What time would you like for Carl and I to have it home tonight?" At that point, Carl's mom must have gotten sick because she jumped up from the table and ran into the bedroom and slammed the door. I looked at Irvin. He was holding his chicken and looking over his glasses at me.

"Jerry," he said, "I believe you and Carl better plan on staying home tonight!"

It was at that point that I found out that that '39 pickup had a second distinct disadvantage: when you brought it home with one side missing, you lost 100 percent of your negotiating power.

But in spite of all that and a million other similar episodes, I still had the greatest time growing up, and I believe that was for three reasons: 1) I had the greatest parents in the world, 2) my parents raised me in the greatest community in the world, and 3) we all have the greatest God a world could want. God bless you all. See you in church in the morning. I've got to get back to the wedding reception. Good night!

33

"The Gift of Compassion"

Browning Junior High Athletic Banquet

May, 1993

Good evening. Thank you for letting me come to be a part of your evening. You may be asking yourself why I am here tonight?" I read the story in the Springfield paper about your school—your basketball team and Jason, and I called Coach Page and told him how much it touched me.

It brought back a lot of memories for me, especially about junior high basketball players and times of grief. Also, it was of special interest to me because it was about the Browning and Fredrick communities. I come through Browning on the way to the Fredrick landing probably about thirty times a year, put in the river and go upstream a mile or so to a cabin and set on the porch and watch the river go by, or maybe in November try to fool a duck or two.

So—here we are tonight, the last Browning Junior High Athletic Banquet, and one of the players, one of your friends, one of your team members, and yes, one of your family is not here with you. We can look around and say, "Is this all there is? Our school is falling off piece by piece—and Jason is gone. What's to look forward to? Life just isn't worth the effort. I can't wait until I get my driver's license. I'm gonna quit school and I'm out of here." That certainly is one option. Let's leave that option for a moment—we'll come back to it later.

Just a minute ago I said the story in the paper brought back a lot of memories for me about junior high basketball players. Give me a few minutes and let me tell you why I wanted to be here and why I feel very close to you, even though I do not know your names. A few years ago during corn harvest, my two sons, Todd, sixteen, and Tim, fourteen, came to the field after school to plow. Before they left the house, they ate supper so they could work late. On the way to the field, they went around a curve on a gravel road and lost control, ending up rolling the van over. Vicki received a call from the neighbors and when she got to the accident, Todd was okay, but Tim was lying on the ground.

When I got there, the neighbors had called the ambulance, so the ambulance soon arrived and took him first to Lincoln, and they said he needed to go to Springfield. The doctor there told us he had hit the dash with his chest and his esophagus had burst. All of those chicken and noodles were scattered in his chest. They operated on him for five hours, trying to take out all they could and then sewed his esophagus back together. For the next eight days he had nothing to eat or drink. He was on a ventilator, so he wrote messages to us and said he wanted to get well because basketball practice started soon.

His recovery seemed to be going well and they moved him out of intensive care. After eight days they gave him a drink of grape juice to see if it would go down or show up in his chest. His esophagus was not healing and the grape juice went into his chest. He got very sick and they took him back into intensive care. After they got him moved, he said, "I think I'm going to die, but I'm not afraid."

It was harvest time so I stayed with him during the night and Vicki came in the daytime. Two days after he was back in intensive care, they came and got me at 4:00 a.m. and said he was getting worse and they were going to operate again. I called Vicki and she soon arrived and then other family members and friends came. We all gathered in the chapel to hope and pray, and when we finished with our prayer, I looked up and saw the doctor standing in the door. He came to us and said, "We lost him." I never saw Tim play a high school game.

So, yes, the story of your basketball team and Jason brought back a flood of memories for me, and yes, I wanted to be with you tonight. Why? Because I have to encourage you, in your own time, to go on. Maybe Vicki and I aren't much of an example, but we are living witnesses that, with the help of your friends and classmates, your team members, your coach and your teachers, your family, your neighbors, and God, you can go on. And how? By forgetting Jason and going on with your life? No. No. No. By remembering Jason and going on with your life.

Tim gave us a gift. Jason gave you a gift. He gave you a gift that many people search a whole lifetime for and never find—and you have it already. What did he give you? He gave you compassion—compassion toward one another. He gave you kindness toward one another. And how did Jason give you that? He showed you through his death that life is sometimes too rough to go it alone, maybe even impossible. He showed you how you need each other in your sufferings and your troubles that you experienced when you first heard about Jason. He showed you through his death what life is really all about: helping and caring and strengthening each other. You can't know that unless you have been helped and cared for yourself through impossible times.

Also, in his death, Jason showed you how precious and delicate and important life is. Never again will you take life for granted. Never again can you honestly say, "I don't need anyone." Jason gave you a gift that money can't buy, and wise men can't teach you. You obtain this gift of compassion only by realizing you need it yourself from others. Another key word to go along with compassion is motivation. Did you know that because you live in this country, you can be almost anything you want to be? I didn't know that when I was your age. I thought if you wanted to be a teacher or a lawyer or doctor, you had to have a special gift or a calling. Well, you do. You have to have the gift of motivation. You know how you get that? It's not very hard. You simply have to want to.

We live along a highway and several years ago, this car came sliding across the highway right up into our yard. I ran out of the shop and up to the car, where I found a very frightened young black girl.

I said, "Are you okay?"

She said, "I think so."

I helped her out of her car and into the house and while we were waiting for the wrecker, I asked her where she lived and where she was going. She said she lived in Peoria and was on her way back to Lincoln College. "I have a scholarship there," she said. "Someday I'm going to be a lawyer."

There is no doubt in my mind that somewhere out there that lady is practicing law.

Motivation. That's all you really need, just to say, "I want to." Then you combine that with the gift of compassion that Jason gave you and you have it all. Compassion is the difference between ordinary people and great people. "Okay," you say, "so Jason gave us compassion. I can even see some good coming from all this. That's good for us, but what about Jason? Why should he have to miss out on life and school and sports?" I can't answer that. I wish I could. But please let me give you a few closing comments.

I think it's only fair to tell you that I believe in God. I'm not here tonight to tell you you have to believe as I do. That's not why I'm here. But after Tim died, this was really a big question for me, and I wasn't getting any answer. I prayed a lot about it. I could see good coming from Tim's death. His friends were thinking a lot about their own life and I wasn't taking my other kids for granted. All of us could see how precious and delicate and extremely important life is, and Tim had given us all that. But what about Tim? What was he doing?

I was sure there was life after death, but what was it? Where was it? What went on there? I couldn't see Tim just sitting around singing songs or something. He loved to play ball. He was voted the most valuable player on his junior high basketball team. He loved to ride motorcycles. He liked action. I went through a couple of months with this constantly on my mind. What's Tim doing? Show me something, God, anything, please. Let me know he's okay.

Nothing—nothing ever happened. And then one night I had a dream. Now it wasn't a vision or anything. It was just an ordinary dream like you might dream. In my dream there was a cornfield and everyone around the cornfield was frightened. When I was a little boy, my mother always said to stay out of the cornfield! You'll get lost in there and we never will find you. In my dream someone was lost in the cornfield. All of a sudden out of the field came two people: a young man about twenty-one and a boy about fourteen. As I ran toward them, I saw that they were both Tim. One as a young man, and one as Tim was when he died. The older Tim was holding the younger Tim's hand and they were both so happy. As I walked to them, the older Tim said, "Dad, look! Look, Dad. I found myself." It was just a dream, but in that dream, Tim was so happy, so complete. I never worried about him again.

So wonderful, wonderful young people of Browning. Where do you go from here? Remember the first option, that's one way. The other way: go on to graduation—to Rushville. Be what you want to be—in school, in sports, in life. And never, never forget: you have a gift, a very special gift that Jason gave you. You have compassion.

Congratulations on your superior basketball season both this year and last. Congratulations on the awards you received tonight. Our athletic director at Hartsburg-Emden, Mr. Dave McGraw, sends his warmest wishes to you, Coach Page. Also, the junior high coach, Ron Spencer, and all the junior high basketball team told me to convey to you that they think of you often and wish you the very best. Coach Page, thank you for letting me come. I'm looking forward to reading great things about these very special young people.

34

"Suffering Is Not Wasted"

Hartsburg Cemetery

Memorial Day—1993

For most of us, Memorial Day is a day of remembering, a day to be thankful, yet a day when we feel sad and lonely. The dictionary says Memorial Day is a U.S. holiday observed in most states on May 30, honoring the dead of the armed forces, also called Decoration Day.

When Don Asher asked me to talk here today, I was kind of reluctant, because we are here to remember those who have gone before us, and especially those who have made the supreme sacrifice on the battlefield—those who gave so unselfishly so those of us left behind could enjoy a better world, a place to live and raise our families in freedom. I didn't help with that task, but I've certainly been a recipient of the fruits of their labor and their pain and suffering, and for that I am most grateful. Maybe it would be okay for someone like me to talk here today.

As I tried to put a few short thoughts together for us to think about to show our respect and gratitude here today, one word kept coming into my mind. The word was suffering. I don't like to think about suffering, none of us do, yet it is a part of life or will be for most of us. Very few of us will escape this life without some suffering—maybe a lot of suffering.

Most, if not all, of those we are remembering today have suffered. Why have they suffered? Why is there so much suffering and sickness in the world? Why are people in far-off countries like Bosnia suffering today? Why did those who gave their lives in wars and conflicts have to suffer? I don't know, but I do know suffering is a part of life. I don't think that I have ever met or even heard of a great man or great woman who hasn't suffered. Nothing seems to build character and wisdom like suffering. James 1:12 says, *"Blessed is the man who endures trial, for when he has stood the test he will receive the crown of life which God has promised to those who love Him."*

When I personally think of suffering, I often think of my son, Tim, who is buried just down the path here. After an auto accident, Tim lay in the hospital seven days without as much as a drink of water. Because of his injury, he was not allowed to swallow anything. After the seventh day, he got a couple swallows of grape juice. They were hoping his injury had healed enough, but it hadn't. He contracted peritonitis and four days later, after much suffering, he died.

Several years ago our whole family was in Washington, DC. We went to Arlington Cemetery to watch the changing of the guard at the Tomb of the Unknown Soldier. No one even knows the name of the person buried there. Surely he suffered. We went to the great wall, the monument that lists the names of the men killed in Vietnam. There are columns and columns of names. Look at the flags waving in the wind here in the cemetery—again suffering. So much suffering.

Why all this suffering and dying in these different places? What is the purpose? While we were planting corn a couple of weeks ago, I heard a really good sermon on the tractor radio on II Corinthians 12:9. Paul told God about his thorn in the flesh three times and God said, *"My grace is sufficient for you, for my power is made perfect in weakness"*. In talking about God's grace being sufficient for us, we are talking about suffering, and this scripture gives us the assurance that *no suffering* is ever wasted. God knows our suffering and whether he caused it or let it happen, or we caused it, God will not let our suffering be wasted, but use it for his glory and his will.

How can he do that? That's the kind of God we have. What do most of us fear most in life? It's suffering and death, isn't it? Yet God in his wisdom takes the thing we fear the most and turns it into the glorious entrance into his presence. No suffering is ever wasted! Somehow, somewhere, it will be used for good and for God!

How can that be? How do I know that? I just know that God said his grace is sufficient. He knows we will suffer and he still says my grace is sufficient for you. But how can we be sure those fallen brothers and sisters we are honoring today didn't die in vain? My friends, even though there is much trouble and suffering in the world today, never, in most of our lifetimes, I know not in mine, have more people been free and independent. Each time a person suffered or died on the battlefield, another country, another group of people, another person was that much closer to freedom.

Communism is dead. Men and women died so others may be free, and more and more men, women, and children are enjoying their freedom today. *"No greater love has a man than to lay down his life for his brother."* That's what fighting for freedom is all about. No, suffering is never wasted. "But we loved them," you say. "What is their reward? We got freedom, but what about them? What is their reward?"

In closing let me read you a few lines from this book called *Prayers*. The part I want to share with you is entitled "*The Funeral*." The preface starts by saying, for a Christian, death does not exist, or rather, it is only a starting point and not an end. The church sings at Masses for the dead, "*Life is not taken away, it is changed.*" In John, Jesus says, "*I am the resurrection and I am life*" (11:25). "*In very truth I tell you, if anyone obeys my teaching he shall never know what it is to die*" (8:51). "*I am that living bread . . . if anyone eats this bread he shall live forever*" (6:51).

The Funeral: People were following. The family, some crying, some pretending to cry; friends, some grieving, some bored or chatting. Leaving the cemetery, some of the family was sobbing, "All is finished." Others were sniffling, "Come, come, my dear, courage: it's finished!" And I was thinking that everything was just beginning. Yes, he had finished the last rehearsal, but the play was just beginning. The years of training were over, but the eternal work was about to start. He had just been born to life, the real life, life that's going to last, life eternal.

As if there were dead people! There are no dead people, Lord. There are only the living, on earth and beyond. Death exists, Lord, but it's nothing but a moment, a second, a step, the step from provisional to permanent, from temporal to eternal, as in the death of the child the adolescent is born, from the caterpillar emerges the butterfly, from the grain the full-blown sheath.

But where are they, Lord, those that I have loved? Are they in ecstasy, taken up with holy loving in harmony with the Trinity? Lord, my loved ones are near me, I know that they live in the spirit. My eyes can't see them because they have left their bodies for a moment, as one steps out of one's clothing. Their souls, deprived of their bodily vesture, no longer communicate with me.

But in you, Lord, I hear them calling me, I see them beckoning to me, I hear them giving me advice, for they are now more vividly present. Before, our bodies touched, but not our souls. Now I meet them when I meet you. I receive them when I receive you. I love them when I love you. Oh, my loved ones, eternally alive, who live in me, help me to learn thoroughly in this short life how to live eternally.

Lord, I love you, and I want to love you more. It's you who makes love eternal, and I want to love eternally.

Suffering is not wasted! It is used by God. Let us be especially thankful today for those who went ahead of us, who suffered for us, so that we may be free and prosper in this great and beautiful land. Amen.

Footnote: Quoist, Michel, *Prayers*, (Avon Books, A division of The Hearst Corporation, New York), pages 40-43.

Part V

Dedication

35. Camp Griesheim Christian Retreat Center Chapel..................211

35

"Camp Griesheim Christian Retreat Center"

Dedication—June 1, 1975

Welcome to Camp Griesheim Christian Retreat Center. It is truly our pleasure to be able to share this day with you. The Board has decided against any long formal dedication service, so this dedication will be very brief.

First of all, I would like to introduce the Retreat Center Board: Dean Bruns, Virgil Leesman, Owen Reiners, Pastor Gene Peisker, Ronald Crane, Wendell Teaney, Alice Lessen, Donna Struebing, Marianna Lessen, Rosemary Klokkenga, Mary Lou Klokkenga, and myself, Jerry Crane, serving as chairman.

This place, I'm sure, brings back many memories for many of you. No doubt, some of you have been here in previous years camping, scouting, and hiking.

The last five months have brought forth much time, money, talents, and some tears. A dream has become a reality because of the dedication of hundreds of people with their many gifts, contributions, memorials, hours of labor, and prayers; but I believe, probably the most important single thing that came from the last five months, came from the very first meeting—the purpose. Why do this? What's the purpose?

I want to read once again the purpose of Camp Griesheim Christian Center: *To share the Gospel of Jesus Christ and enjoy the pleasures of nature in a constructive Christian atmosphere.*

There's been a lot of work on this project. Yesterday, at one time, I counted fifty-six people here, cleaning, scrubbing, painting, even wiring, plumbing, yes, even nailing walls together in the shower rooms. The carpenters said it was the first time they were ever followed so closely with a paintbrush. Concrete blocks were laid yesterday on the shower room entrance.

All this for what? to help fulfill this purpose: to share the Gospel of Jesus during the months and years that follow. If anyone comes to this place with his church or the scouts and is unable to experience Christ's love through people, nature, or some other way, then this board has failed and our purpose has failed.

It is our sincere hope and prayer that this retreat center will be a place where your church, a part of the church—Christ's church—can be glorified and strengthened; because it was out of the love for his church that this idea was born. We don't need new and different programs, we just need to get behind the ones that are already there, because it's the church that down through the years has kept the Gospel of Jesus Christ alive.

Those who have been involved here—how can we thank you enough? We wish, now that the building is almost complete, that it could be used free of charge, but we feel that would be almost impossible. There certainly will be upkeep and maintenance, utilities and fees, which must be paid out; so we have come up with a small rate chart, which you will find on the back of the bulletin you were given.

Hopefully, over the summer, a couple of improvements can be made: the pond down the hill reconstructed, the road improved, and further landscaping.

It's been a great time for those of us who have been involved here. It's been a time of working and praying together, a time of strengthening friendships and relationships, of getting to know each other better. Five months of work, sometimes day and night, and now it's time to dedicate this place.

How do you properly dedicate this retreat center? It was planned, engineered, financed and constructed for one purpose: to share the love and the Gospel of Jesus. So, to him it will be dedicated. May this place be some very small token of thanking him for what he did for us. We will dedicate this place to him in prayer. Let's stand now and pray.

Lord Jesus, how we stand in awe at the beauty of this place that you have created! How we praise you for sharing it with us! You truly are a great and wonderful God! Lord, we ask for your forgiveness for any anxieties or hardships or frustrations that may have been caused through the construction of this place. As honest as we can possibly be, it was done in love. We thank you for this and for the sunshine and all those who came. We thank you for the money and the time that you gave to this place.

We pray for our churches, Lord, that in some way this place may be a benefit to you through your church. We pray for the people who worked here and who gave of themselves, but most of all, we pray for those who will come here. Be with all those here as they return later today to their homes.

And now, Lord Jesus, we, in whatever capacity we have, give this building, this place, to you. It is yours, just as we are, to use as you see fit. We thank you, we praise you, and we love you. We now dedicate and turn this place completely over to you, Jesus, our Savior and our Lord. Amen.

Footnote:

In 1979, board members saw a need for a bigger area for worship. Volunteers built an A-frame chapel. Now steps on the deck lead down to the chapel, which has enough folding chairs to seat one hundred people. A red carpet covers the chapel floor and a pulpit has been erected at the far end of the building. Behind the pulpit is a clear glass window, allowing a view of the trees outside.

Jerry said, "The whole idea was to get out here to enjoy nature. We didn't put in an altar. We figured the trees were an altar. When I was a kid, there were no deer or turkeys here; however, since the retreat center began, both deer and turkeys have returned, and smaller animals, such as squirrels and raccoons, abound on the twenty-one-acre plot."

A path leads down the hill from the parking lot to a bridge, and across the bridge are a rustic cross and a bench for those who wish to sit and meditate.

Jerry served as president of the Board of Directors of the Camp Griesheim Christian Retreat Center from its inception in 1975 until his death on January 16, 2006.

In the past thirty-three years, there have been 1,604 events held at Camp Griesheim Christian Retreat Center involving 42,372 people.

Part VI

Weddings

36. "Grace-Filled Love" 217
37. "Love Never Fails" 221
38. "An Eight-Cow Wife" 225
39. "Blessing on Marriage" 229

36

"Grace-Filled Love"

Today you're getting married. Your family and your friends are all here. Probably never before in your life have you had so many people around you who love and care for you. It's a perfect day. May God bless you both.

The Gospel you have chosen for today is from Matthew, chapter 19, beginning with the fourth verse. In this text Jesus is talking to a group of people called the Pharisees. They were hoping to trick him into taking a stand on divorce, but Jesus in his wisdom focused not on divorce, but on marriage, for his answer. Jesus speaks, *"Haven't you read the scripture that says, 'In the beginning the Creator made male and female, and God said, For this reason a man will leave his father and mother and join to his wife, and the two shall become one flesh. So they are no longer two, but one flesh. What therefore God has joined together let not man put asunder.'?"*

It looks to me like a miracle is about to take place here. Two people are about to become one. Soon you will be husband and wife and you will light the unity candle together, signifying you are now one.

I don't know exactly what kind of change is going to take place, but rest assured, Jesus is talking more than physical here. You are individuals, but from this day, everything you do, and everything you think, will be influenced by the other. Yet you have not lost your freedom, you have gained the freedom to love and respond to each other's love. That's the way the Creator designed life and from this day forward, you are free to live in that relationship.

When I was asked to speak at your wedding, I thought and thought about what I could say that might be meaningful. I couldn't come up with anything that seemed just right. Then the other day in Sunday school, I heard a man on a tape and he was talking about a play that he had seen some time ago called, *"Raisin in the Sun,"* written by Loraine Handelberry. What he said seemed really good to me and I thought it just might fit for today. I remembered the play had been made into a movie, so I went to see if it was available. At the second video store I found it—a two-part video, 171 minutes long. I brought it home and was intrigued by it, because, in my opinion, it was really about relationships: our relationship with God and our relationship with others. I believe relationships are what give life meaning and purpose.

Maybe some of you saw the play or the movie. *"Raisin in the Sun"* is the story of a black family living in a poor neighborhood in a crowded apartment. The father died, but through struggling and saving all his life, he leaves about $10,000 to the family in the way of a legacy. The mother, Lena, says this money is going to allow her to fulfill her dream. And what is her dream? A small house away from there with window boxes and flowers, and sunlight that actually hits the backyard, where she can plant a garden.

The married son of the household begs for the money. This young man, who never had a chance, never had a break, never had a good job—he has a friend, and with this friend and the money, they could go into business. They have a deal going, and they can make a lot of money and do good things for the family. They could soon buy an even better house. He begs and pleads and his mother doesn't want to give him the money, but how can she deny her son, her boy, who never had a chance? So, she gives him the money, and you can guess what happened.

The friend takes the money and leaves town, and when the son, Walter Lee, finally realizes the money is gone, he is beaten and battered. He is utterly destroyed. His sister, she lights into him. She tears him up, puts him down. She has nothing but contempt for him, having been so stupid to get ripped off like this! The whole family's hopes, their mother's dream, destroyed.

Then, when the son, Walter Lee, leaves, the mother speaks to her daughter. I want to read the script word for word so I can be sure and get it right. Lena, the mother, speaks, *"I thought I taught you to love him."*

"Love him?" the daughter says, *"Love him? There's nothing left to love."*

And Mama says (with love), *"There's always something left to love, and if you ain't learned that, you ain't learned nuthin'. Have you cried for that boy today? I don't mean for you and for the rest of the family 'cause we lost that money. I mean for him and what he's been through and what it's done to him! Child, child, when do you think it's the time to love someone the most? When he's done good and made it easy for everybody? Well, you ain't learned nuthin' 'cause that ain't the time at all. It's when he's at his lowest and can't believe in himself 'cause the world done whipped him so. When you start to measure a man—measure him right, child. Make sure you take into account what hills and valleys he's done come through before he gets to where he's at."*

I don't know what we call that kind of love, but the Bible calls it *grace*. When you don't deserve love and you get love, when you don't deserve to be cared for, and you're cared for—God loves you not just when you've done something good, he loves you all the time, and he creates a love in you that enables you to love that other person, no matter what that person does.

Can you understand that? Can we understand that? Can we do that? No, not always, but if that relationship really matters, then that's our goal! And God—God not only showed us how to respond in relationships, he promises to continue to be with us always to help and to guide us. God bless you on this very special day as the two of you become one.

37

"Love Never Fails"

You have chosen a powerful text for your very special day. I Corinthians 13 is referred to by some as a hymn of love. Others call it the love chapter of God's word. I'd like to read again verses 4-7 from chapter 13. Yes, this text is all about love and what love is. On the front of our programs it says, *"Love one another, for love is of God."* Love comes from God. God created love. Without God, there would be no love in this world.

You say you love each other. If that is so, and I believe it is, God has put it there. Let's take the word love, and very briefly, come up with a word for each of its letters that help us to describe it more fully. It might be well for all of us who are married to join in these thoughts.

We'll start with *"L,"* the first letter of love. I would like to use the word *liberates*. Love liberates. It does not bind us. In marriage, we are completely committed, yet liberated. We are free to love each other and to love God. Marriage provides a structure for our lives that sets us free. We are bound only to Christ. We are completely liberated.

For the letter "*O*," the second letter of love, let's use *organize*. No matter how busy your lives may be, organize some time for each other and time to do things you need to do. Without organization, time will slip by, and there won't be enough time for each other. To learn to organize is an important part of love.

For "*V*," *volunteer*. Volunteer means of your own free will. Give your love away freely. Forget your own selfishness. Do things for one another and for God. Love never fails when you give it away. Volunteer.

"*E*," the last letter, *envelop*. Envelop means to cover completely. Envelop yourselves in an environment of God. What does that mean? Put God first in everything. Remember, God created love. You love each other and you want it to grow. Don't start this marriage without God!

I once heard a man say that he was on a plane waiting for take-off. Everything seemed ready, yet they waited and waited. Finally, he asked the flight attendant, "Why the delay?"

"We're waiting for the pilot," she said. "We can't take off without the pilot. If we do, we are certain to crash." Don't take off without the pilot. God is the creator of love. He's the pilot.

L-O-V-E. Henry H. Halley, in his well-known commentary, says love is the most powerful ultimate force in the universe, and everything else, yes, everything, is only temporary without it.

Let all of us remember the text that was chosen for this very special day for it says, "*I may be able to speak the languages of men and even of angels, but if I have no love, my speech is no more than a noisy gong or a loud bell. I may have the gift of inspired preaching. I may have more knowledge than any man has ever obtained, and I may understand all secrets. I may have enough faith to build a house or move a mountain, but if I have no love, I am nothing. I may give everything I have to the poor, and I may even give my body to be burned for a great cause, but if I have no love, all this does me no good. Love is patient and kind; it is not jealous or conceited or proud. Love is not ill mannered or selfish or irritable. Love does not keep a record of wrongs. Love is not happy with evil, but is happy with the truth. Love never gives up. And its faith and its hopes and its patience will never fail."*

May God bless you both richly. He loves you, and so do all of us gathered here to be with you today.

38

"An Eight-Cow Wife"

Tasha and Uvaldo, I'll tell a little story and then close with a couple of thoughts.

Tasha, your mother came home with a devotional book for a wedding present for you. I sat down in my chair in the kitchen, opened it to the middle and started to read. I read it again and asked her to come sit by me so I could read her a story. It is a simple story and yet has such depth. Here's the story:

This guy—I'll call him Joe—is staying in Japan. He has three-weeks leave so he sailed down into the South Pacific to visit the island of Kinewata. From this island Joe could sail to other islands or just stay there at the main island for a few days. He stayed at an inn and talked to the innkeeper about sailing off to another island the next day. The innkeeper suggested another island, and suggested Joe look up Johnny Lingo. Johnny Lingo wasn't the man's real name, but the innkeeper was from Chicago and he had Americanized the islanders' names and Johnny Lingo stuck. Everyone on the islands knew Johnny Lingo.

It seemed Johnny Lingo had access to everything. He grew vegetables—the greenest, freshest vegetables on the islands. He would trade them for pearls. Johnny was the best trader on the islands, and he was honest. He would say, "Johnny Lingo take care of you 100 percent", and then the innkeeper chuckled. A little boy about Christopher's size was sitting in the hotel. When he heard Johnny Lingo's name he laughed, almost mocking him. Joe remembered talking with other islanders that day, and the name Johnny Lingo had come up, and they all laughed.

Finally, Joe said, "Everyone tells me to get in touch with Johnny Lingo, and then starts to laugh. Let me in on the joke." Well, the innkeeper said that Johnny was the quickest, fastest, strongest man on these islands, but there's one thing. Five months ago during the fall festival, he found himself a wife. He paid eight cows for her.

Joe knew island customs. You could buy a fair wife for one or two cows; a very good wife for four or five, but eight? "Must be a beauty," Joe said.

The innkeeper replied, "Kindest thing you could say about Sarita is plain. She was skinny, walked with shoulders hunched over, head ducked down, scared of her own shadow."

"Then how do you explain eight cows"?

"We can't. That's why the villagers all grin and talk about Johnny. Sharpest trader on the islands taken by Sarita's father."

"Eight cows," Joe said. "Tomorrow I'm sailing to meet Johnny Lingo and his eight-cow wife."

The next day Joe set sail and shortly after noon-time, he docked his boat and started looking for Johnny Lingo. He wasn't hard to find. Everyone knew him and he did have the biggest house on the island. Johnny invited Joe in and Joe instantly asked Johnny about his eight-cow purchase of his bride.

While Joe was talking, Sarita walked into the room. She was no doubt the most beautiful woman Joe had ever seen—the lift of her shoulders, the tilt of her chin, the sparkle in her eyes, her beautiful dark hair—she was gorgeous! After she left the room, Johnny said, "You admire Sarita." "She—she's glorious," said Joe "but this cannot be Sarita from the main island."

"Only one Sarita, but perhaps she does not look the same as she looked on the main island."

"She can't," Joe said. "I heard . . . well . . . homely. All the people make fun of you for letting Sarita's father cheat you."

"Think eight cows too many?"

"No, but how can she be so different?"

"Did you ever think," Johnny asked, "what it must mean to a woman to know her husband settled on the lowest price for which she can be bought? Then later, at the market place, when women talk, what husbands paid: four cows, two cows, one cow. That could not happen to my Sarita."

"Then you did it to make her happy."

"Well, I wanted Sarita to be happy, but I wanted more. You say she is different. This is true. Many things can change a woman. Things that happen inside. Things that happen outside. But what matters most is what she thinks of herself. On the main island, Sarita thought she was worth nothing. Now she knows she is worth more to me than any woman in all the islands."

"Then what did you want, Johnny?"

"I wanted to marry Sarita. I loved her and no other woman." And Johnny said, "I wanted an eight-cow wife."

Tasha, since you've known Uvaldo, you are different. You are brighter, happier, more confident, not because you were purchased for eight cows, but more important, I think, it's because Uvaldo sees tremendous value in you. He's not afraid to be good to you, to be considerate, to respect you. It has been good for your self-worth and confidence.

Tasha, you have done the same for Uvaldo. That's why I'm excited about this marriage. You two have been good to each other and now you're standing here ready to be married. A new life, a fresh start, and that new life is just waiting here for you. You see, Jesus Christ specializes in new beginnings and fresh starts. Every day we start anew. The old is gone and Christ blesses us with the very first day of the rest of our lives.

He died for each one of us. Ephesians 4:2—*"Be humble and gentle; be patient, bearing with one another in love."* If you do that, Uvaldo, you'll have an eight-cow wife, and Tasha, you'll have a husband who deserves and is easy to be loved.

You see, I know about eight-cow wives. In four days I'll have been married forty-three years to an eight-cow wife. God bless you both.

39

"Blessing on Marriage"

―――∽∽∽⋘⋙∽∽∽―――

Tonya and Nathan, you have entitled this part of your celebration as the "Blessing on Marriage." I suppose this could mean a blessing from Vicki and me. It could represent a blessing from all of us here as we rejoice with Tonya and Nathan on this special day.

Maybe it's because I'm your father, Tonya, (But I don't think so, I think it's much bigger than that), but the blessing I see is not only for you two, but for all of us here as we focus on what is happening, what is taking place here in the trees at Camp Griesheim.

This morning I crossed the walk bridge on the other side of the building and I went up by a little altar in the trees to pray. I prayed for you, Tonya and Nathan. I want to share with all of you that prayer. For this prayer, don't close your eyes or bow your heads. Just concentrate your attention on Nathan and Tonya, and what God has done for them through Jesus, and equally important, what Jesus has done or is willing to do for us all. Let's pray—remember, focus on Tonya and Nathan and what God is doing.

Dear God, you are the Father of us all. You sent your son Jesus so that we might be able to approach you, knowing we have your love and forgiveness. Tonya and Nathan are coming to you for a new start, a new life together. Is this possible, Father? Can we dare to ask for such a thing? You are a God of perfection, a God who hates sin. Yet we know somehow, through Jesus, you are able to forgive us and let us start over. Thank you, dear God. Amen.

Is this prayer just empty words? I wondered, is it just a hope, a maybe? Just something to make us feel good for the moment of today? Do we realize what is happening here? Tonya and Nathan, this is your second time. Each of you were married before. God said, "This was not my plan for you, but through what Jesus did for you, please know that I forgive you." I love you, and for whatever reason, God decided to do more than that for you. He said, "I want to give you a chance to be happy. I will give you Nathan, and I will give you Tonya, someone to be happy with." You see, God is more than a God of love and forgiveness. God is a God of *completeness*.

Tonya and Nathan, I look at you today and I see what God has done. It makes me and all of us here realize what an awesome and wonderful God we have.

May God continue to bless us all so richly in his *completeness* as he has blessed you, Nathan and Tonya.

Part VII

Funerals

40. "This Is Not Unto Death, But for the Glory of God"—Tim Crane 233
41. "Your Children Are Your Legacy"—Creston Hildebrands 237
42. "Counting on His Grace"—Steve Westen 239
43. "We Need an Exit Plan"—Cleo Reiners 245
44. "Wind River Canyon"—Jim Bluhm 251
45. "Save Me a Seat, Buzz"—Buzz Davis 255
46. "The Gift"—Bryan Bergman 259
47. "A Tryst with the Master"—Thoughts on Death and Heaven 263
48. "The Ultimate Healing"—Reaching Out to Those Who Are Grieving 269

40

"This Is Not Unto Death, But for the Glory of God"

Tim Crane's Memorial Service

November 3, 1978

―――∽∽∽⌒⌒⌒∽∽∽―――

I suppose it's kind of unusual to have a service like this, but it was the way things turned out that prompted us to want to do something. First of all, so many people have done so much for us, and I didn't know how else to thank you. So many letters and so many prayers have sustained us and kept us going, and Tim knew it.

One day when Tim was feeling a little better, he said, "If everybody is praying for me, how come I'm not getting better?"

Well, those are things we can't answer, but the other day when I went to school and talked to some of his friends, I just felt they needed to know about how Tim lived and how he died. And I thought this could be one way to get everybody together.

At the time of the accident, we went down there and we could see that Tim was having trouble breathing. We had some anxious moments, but they got him going and loaded him up and took him in the ambulance. We started owing people right away from the start, as hard as they worked and all they did, from the neighbors who helped us, to the paramedics, on down the line.

Vicki said, "Jerry, I just thought of a Bible verse that seems so real, it just came to my mind. It's John 11:4."

It was when Jesus was talking about Lazarus. When Jesus heard about Lazarus' death, he said, *"This illness is not unto death. It is for the glory of God so that the Son of Man may be glorified by means of it."* We really clung to that, that it was not unto death. We thought Tim was going to make it right from the beginning.

A lot of people said, "I bet you knew this was going to happen." We really didn't. We thought right from the beginning that Tim was going to make it, and Tim never gave up. He showed us how precious life is, and he worked really hard to hold onto it, extremely hard. And every time they asked him to do something, he did it twice as well. He never complained through all those days, and he never shed a tear. That's how much he thought about life.

But one night, when he got pretty sick, he said, "I'm really sick, Dad."

And I said, "How sick, Tim?"

And he said, "I think I'm going to die."

I said, "You really think that?"

And he said, "I believe I am, but I'm not scared. I'm ready. I'm ready to die, and I'm not scared." But he kept on fighting anyway, and that was the kind of thing that I admired about him. He didn't give up on life, even though he was ready to die, because it was precious to him. He kept saying, "I may miss a few practices, but I'll be back there."

Tim really got ready, and he really got his head together. And when it came time to go, he went. And I really believe that Tim saw something better, as much as he liked it here, as much as he loved you people. That's my thought. I can't tell you if that's true. I don't know. It was like he saw a glimpse of something better, and the way he always did, he ran after that because it was better.

The doctors were almost overwhelmed because they didn't really think he would die. They told us how sorry they were. They just couldn't keep his heart going. But that's the way Tim lived and that's the way Tim died. We asked if we could see him, and they said yes, and so we did. We could tell, just like back there in the casket, that his body is like an old coat that Tim has thrown down and went on. He has no use for that body anymore.

And you kids, thinking about this, don't worry about seeing it go into the ground, because it's no good anymore. Don't worry about Tim, because he's okay. I think we kind of feel a little sorry for ourselves once in a while, and I don't feel a bit ashamed about that, not a bit, and don't you either. We go right on, and we think about him, and you talk about him all you want to, but don't worry about Tim. I don't want you to forget that, you kids. Don't worry about Tim.

Once again, I really want to thank you so much. For those of you who can come to the funeral tomorrow, we invite you to come. We're going to keep the same theme: *To God be the glory*. Pastor Spenn is going to be preaching on Ephesians 3:20-21. This is what we believe. We believe this very much. So many people said that we prayed so hard, but our prayers were not answered. We believe this verse: *"Now to him who by the power at work within us is able to do far more abundantly than all that we ask or think, to him be glory in the church and in Christ Jesus to all generations, for ever and ever."* He answered our prayers above and beyond what we ever dreamed of.

Once more, thank you so much for coming.

41

"Your Children Are Your Legacy"

Funeral Sermon for Creston Hildebrandt

July 22, 1996

To those of you who love Creston, my wife, Vicki, and I want to convey our heartfelt sympathy to you. His loss is one that at times will seem almost unbearable as you miss his physical presence with you. It's hard, really hard, but it's what happens when we love someone and they go ahead of us. May God be with you in your grief.

A little over sixty-eight years ago, a baby boy was born to Harm and Rosie Hildebrandt. Wouldn't it be great if we could know what they were thinking when they first looked at that baby? What Harm and Rosie's dreams might have been for this baby they called Creston as they thought about his life ahead?

When Nancy told me that Creston was very sick, Vicki and I wanted to go and visit with him. Little did we realize what a short time he had left here. While we visited, we reminisced and remembered, talked about things of earlier days. I remembered one winter I washed cars in Emden and Creston would bring his station wagon in to get washed. Every square inch of those windows would be covered with fingerprints, and I would find all kinds of things under the seats. That station wagon hauled as many kids as some school buses.

Years later, Creston moved the family half a mile down the road from where Vicki and I live. He was proud to purchase that home and fix it up. He especially enjoyed his family, cars, yard, and garden there. When it used to snow a lot, I'd hear the Hildebrandt kids go home at night and I'd say, "I don't think they'll make it through the snow drift," and pretty soon there would be a knock at the door and we'd get the tractor or pickup out and drive through the snow to pull them out.

Creston told me the other day he had worked on his will, and with tears in his eyes, he said, "Jerry, I'm not going to have much left."

"Oh, Creston," I said, "your legacy is your children. Your money went to raise kids." Every holiday we would see the cars, vans, pickups, and motorcycles head down the road to Creston and Eva's, and we'd say the traffic jam is starting. The kids are coming home. And they would eat and sit in the yard and play ball, and Creston would watch the grandkids play. You can't put a money value on that.

In the Bible in Matthew 16:26, Jesus said, *"What will it profit a man if he gains the whole world and forfeits his life!"* Yes, you children and grandchildren, you are your father's and mother's legacy. May God bless you as you live out your lives remembering what your parents gave you, and even now, in the midst of trouble and heartache, remember how your Lord has blessed you.

42

"Counting on His Grace"

Steve Westen's Funeral

April 7, 2005

Steven L. Westen was born December 25, Christmas Day, 1950, in Lincoln, Illinois, the son of Irene Westen. Steve died at 10:05 p.m. April 4, 2005, in St. John's Hospice in Springfield, Illinois. He was fifty-four years, three months, and ten days old. He had been ill two weeks. Steve was a self-employed carpenter in Emden and had also been a carpenter in Naples, Florida.

He is survived by his mother, Irene, and also uncles and aunts, Loren and Shirley Westen, Bud and Anna Westen, and numerous cousins. He was preceded in death by his grandparents and his Aunt Fauline and Uncle Alfred Johnson, and his Aunt Agnes and Uncle Virgil Marten. Steve spent a lot of time growing up with his uncles and aunts and cousins.

When Irene asked me to say a few words about Steve, I was really honored. Several years ago Steve and I worked together on the farm. One winter we built a fireplace in our house there on the curve north of Hartsburg. That was where I first heard the famous Westen saying: "Nobody asked how long it took, just who did it." Later I heard Bud and Lornie say the same thing, and I figured it must have come from Grandpa Westen.

Steve was a perfectionist with his carpenter work. He was never satisfied until it was as perfect as he could get it. A good example was the room he built on Aaron and Dena Bergman's house. If you've never seen it, stop sometime and ask Aaron and Dena to show it to you. He really liked restoring old things like the wheel on Jim and Joyce Klokkenga's windmill.

Steve liked to read books on history and he liked to watch the History and Discovery channels on TV. He liked to laugh and reminisce about trips he had taken with Roger Mammen and Randy Wagner. While he was in Naples, Florida, working for an older couple, they took a liking to Steve and offered him an apartment above their garage that they had all fixed up. Steve laughed when they told some of their friends that Steve was their nephew.

I wondered what else I would like to say about Steve, and I thought, "Should I say what I think Irene wants me to say? Should I say what his friends would want me to say, or what his family would want me to say?" I finally decided last night at 9 o'clock I think I'm going to say what I think Steve would want me to say to you if he could speak to you right now. Now that's hard to do, and it has to be what I know to be the truth, so I'm going to share with you three memories that I have with Steve, memories that I think tell me down deep who Steve was and that I think he would want you to know about him. If you have a different idea, then you think of the memories that you have with Steve that are meaningful to you.

After my son died, I looked Steve up and talked to him about Tim. I told him he had died and I wanted Steve to come to the funeral. Steve said he just couldn't. I said, "I want you to."

I remember he stared at the ground and he said, "I can't. I just can't, but I'll tell you what I'm going to do. I'm going to go to a place where Tim loved to be and stay there during the funeral."

I said, "That's good enough for me."

When I left the cemetery after the funeral, I drove down Route 121 and there was Steve's car out in the field by the pond where Tim and Todd always swam. I could see Steve sitting on the diving platform that Moe and Owen and Bob Eeten had built. He was just sitting there staring in the water. He stayed until we left the cemetery. What does that say about a man? Does it say he was hurt, that he was sad, that he had compassion? Was he wondering why things happen? You decide. It made me think that Steve cared for Vicki and me and our family.

Secondly, I think Steve would want me to say to you, "I loved my mother." When Irene was sick, Steve and I talked. He told me how much his mother had wrong with her. I said, "Steve, this is pretty scary. What if they didn't get it all? What if it comes back? What if she dies?"

"I don't know," he said. "Mother's always been there. I can't imagine life without her." Yes, Irene. Steve loved his mother.

Then there was the time I asked Steve to go to Kogudus with me in Urbana—a three-day Christian retreat. "Oh, I don't know about that," Steve said. "That's pretty confining. If I don't like it, I can't leave. I won't have a car if I go with you. I don't know. I don't think so." Steve was working with us then, so I told Vicki to see if she could talk him into it. So the next day after she fixed Steve and me a big dinner, she started talking to him. He never said a word as Vicki continued on. Finally he said, "If you want me to go that bad, I'll go." So Steve and Owen and I took off a few days later for Urbana.

The first night everyone had gone to bed and the three of us met in a room they were using for a chapel. We were talking about the day and Steve said, "You know, a beer sure would taste good right now." It was real cold outside, but I told Owen to open the window and look on the ledge. I had hid a six-pack outside on the window sill. We sat there and talked until two o'clock in the morning. We drank a little beer and talked about the ways and the words of Jesus Christ and what they meant for us. It was a great night for me and I think it was for Steve and Owen.

On Sunday there was a commitment service at the church and everyone was supposed to make a commitment. I remember wondering what Steve would do. Finally, Steve got up and walked to the altar and knelt down, and the pastor said, "Steve, Christ is counting on you."

Steve said, "And I on his grace." And I on his grace. Can you think of anything better to say? What else can we say except I'm counting on your grace?

It's my guess that Steve said it again last Monday night at 10:05 p.m. It's all I'll be able to say—it's all you'll be able to say. We all need a Savior and we've all got one. Jesus died for our sins. All we have to do is believe it. (Romans 8:37-38)

When Steve was in the hospice unit, Irene stepped out in the hallway for a moment and noticed a poem hanging on the wall. She read it and liked it, and wanted me to read it today. Anita wrote it down and Maralee typed it up.

"I'M FREE"

Don't grieve for me for now I'm free;
I'm following the path God laid for me.
I took His hand when I heard Him call;
I turned my back and left it all.
I could not stay another day
To laugh, to love, to work, to play.
Tasks left undone must stay that way;
I've found that peace at the close of day.
If my parting has left a void—
Then fill it with remembered joy:
A friendship shared, a laugh, a kiss;
Oh, yes, these things I too will miss.
Be not burdened with times of sorrow;
I wish you the sunshine of tomorrow.
My life's been full, I've savored much:
Good friends, good times, my loved one's touch.
Perhaps my time seemed all too brief;
Don't lengthen it now with undue grief.
Lift up your heart and share with me,
God wanted me now! He set me free!

Anne Davison 1974

43

"We Need an Exit Plan"

Cleo Reiners' Funeral

August 25, 2005

Cleo Reiners was born April 25, 1918. He was the first child of Edward and Etta Zimmer Reiners. Cleo has one sister, LuAnn. He married Ruth Culleton on February 8, 1950, in Lincoln. Ruth died about nine months ago on November 9, 2004. They were married over fifty-four years.

Cleo served his country in the U.S. Army during World War II. Among other places, he served in Italy, Africa, England, and Germany. He left home for the army in 1940 and never returned until 1945. He was away from home for five years.

Besides being a farmer, Cleo was a carpenter. He worked at the Emden Lumber Yard and built many barns and corn cribs in the Emden area. He also worked on several homes. Cleo was Orvil Township Road Commissioner from 1967 to 1981, and then worked with his son, Dick, for another eleven years for a total of twenty-five years working on the roads in Orvil Township.

Cleo died at 4:00 p.m. on Monday, August 22, 2005, at Abraham Lincoln Memorial Hospital. He had lived approximately eleven months at the Mason City Nursing Home prior to his death.

There is a tombstone in Hartsburg Cemetery that says on the back:*Our children are Diane, Gary, Owen, Tom, Becky, Carl, Dick, Betty Jo, Lee, and Carrie.* What a legacy for Cleo and Ruth. It might be easy to say that Cleo let all his kids do whatever they wanted, and gave them whatever money they wanted to spend, however they wanted to spend it, and they didn't have to work for it, but it wouldn't be exactly true. In fact, it wouldn't be true at all. Cleo ran a tight ship, and everyone had to work, and no one was allowed to waste anything. That's the way it was. There wasn't a board thrown away and there wasn't any food wasted. Sometimes Cleo even kept the used nails. He knew if you were going to raise ten kids on a Scully lease, you had to be cautious. But there was always plenty of food in Cleo and Ruth's kitchen.

There were always all kinds of animals on the farm to be taken care of and they supplied all the meat, milk, and eggs. This made for a lot of work taking care of them, and Saturday, when the boys were home from school, was the day to clean the chicken house. With all the kids and all those animals, there were a lot of stories that developed through the years. Now, I can't tell a story about every one of you kids or we would be here all day, but maybe just a couple of stories.

Owen had caught a pheasant and raised it into a really nice bird. One night he overheard Cleo telling Ruth that he thought that pheasant was about ready to butcher. Owen couldn't bear to think about everyone eating his pet pheasant, so early the next morning, Owen got up and took his pheasant and put him over the fence, figuring he would go on out through the lot and into the field to live happily ever after. But the pheasant was so tame he just stood there and an old sow walked by and before Owen could get over the fence, the sow ate the pheasant right before Owen's eyes. So much for protecting the pheasant.

Then there was the time when Barney had chores in the chicken house, but he had to cross a lot to get there, and in the lot was a turkey that would chase Barney and try to peck him. Barney didn't want to do his chores, but Cleo told him he had to figure something out and do his work. Later on they looked out and they saw this big cardboard box sliding across the yard up to the gate. Two hands came out of the box and opened the gate and the box started sliding across the lot toward the chicken house. It was Barney in the box trying to camouflage himself from the turkey.

Yes, Cleo ran a tight ship, but in the process, he taught his kids how to work and how to figure things out to make them work. He taught them how to build things and how not to waste anything. But you can't remember Cleo without remembering Ruth. Ruth was compassionate and strong and she worked hard. Life wasn't always easy for Cleo and Ruth. They buried two sons, Gary and Tex, but it seemed in some ways this made them stronger and they used these tough times in their lives to help others.

I remember when Vicki and I came home from the hospital after our son died. We walked into the house and Ruth was standing at our kitchen sink washing dishes. She had already heard that Tim had died and she knew how we were feeling. It wasn't easy for her to pray with us and it wasn't easy for her to sit and cry with us, but she did what she knew best. She came and went to work, and when we walked into the kitchen that day, she turned and said, "You think you won't live through this, but you will," and she went back to work. I knew she understood.

A few days after the funeral, I saw Cleo out by our grain bins with the township truck. I went out to see what he was doing. Cleo said,

"I had been thinking you need a wider culvert here. I'll put it in for you." Then as he stepped into the truck, he turned and said, "If there's anything else . . ."

So, Reiners' kids—maybe there were times you might have wished things were different, more material things, maybe less work. But remember, you have something few people have—the closeness and the memories of a big family. You have had experiences most of us can't even comprehend. You are almost the end of an era—raising a large family on a real family farm.

I want to close with one more story. Cleo always tried to watch over his animals, and one thing that really got him upset was when something would get in the chicken house and kill his chickens. A couple of mornings, Cleo or Ruth had gone to the chicken house and found dead chickens. Something was killing the chickens. Well, a couple of nights later, Cleo heard something in the chickens and he took off for the chicken house, slowing down only long enough to pick up a ball bat on the way. Cleo got to the chicken house door, stepped in and turned on the light. There in the middle of the chicken house was a big tomcat standing over a chicken he had just killed.

The cat looked at Cleo and took off for the back corner, but there was no way out there. He went to the other corner, still no way out. By this time the chickens were going crazy and the place was full of dust and chicken feathers. The only way out was the door behind Cleo. The cat made a bolt for the door. Cleo took a swing and missed and the cat went around the chicken house as fast as he could go and made another lunge for the door. The cat made several laps, but you all know the outcome. Cleo came out of the chicken house door, ball bat in one hand, cat in the other.

Why would I tell this story? I've heard it so many times over the years. I thought about it a lot yesterday, and I thought, you know, that cat made two major mistakes. Number one, he had no plan for his exit, and number two, he forgot who was lord of the chicken house.

As I thought about this, I said to myself, "I'm just like that cat. I'm so tied up with life and what I want, I forget that someday I'll need an exit plan, and again like the cat, I sometimes forget who's lord of the chicken house, or in my case, who's Lord of my life." Jesus says in John 14:6, "*I am the way, the truth, and the life. No one can come to the Father except through me.*"

So Diane, Owen, Becky, Carl, Dick, Betty Jo, Barney, and Carrie, your spouses, your children, and all of us here, we too need a plan, and guess what? God's already provided the plan. We just need to be a part of it, and remember that Jesus is the Lord of our life. That's our treasure. And don't forget the other treasure God gave you: the treasure of being raised in a large family with real people. God bless all the Reiners and your families and your memories. Amen.

44

"Wind River Canyon"

Graveside Service for Jim Bluhm

October 7, 1985

———∿∽⚬↶⚬⚭⚬↷⚬∽∿———

Dorothy asked me if I would say a few words here at Jim's grave. We are here because we want to be. We want to be of some comfort, if at all possible, for one another, for those of you who were extra close to Jim, those of you who lived with him and loved him, and especially Dorothy, for you and Valerie, who shared the home on the lake across the street for many years together, and your families. May God's comfort come to you.

In August of 1979, I was able to attend a retreat with Jim at Camp Griesheim Christian Retreat Center, about thirty-five miles south of here. We got together on a Friday evening with about thirty other men. We ate together and kind of got to know one another better during the evening. Saturday we studied together, and what we studied was the Apostles' Creed. Let me read to you the Creed that Jim studied. (Read Creed).

On the next day, Sunday, each man had an opportunity to come forward to make a commitment, if he wanted to. I remember I was standing by the pastor, and as Jim knelt, the pastor said to Jim, "Jim, Christ is counting on you!"

And Jim responded, "And I on his grace." And I on his grace. What else could you say? What else is there that we can depend on or hang our hopes on—the grace of Jesus Christ. Jim couldn't depend on being good enough. Just like you and me, Jim was a sinner. He wasn't perfect. But remember the last part of that creed that Jim studied? "I believe in the Holy Spirit, the Holy Christian Church, the communion of saints, the forgiveness of sins, the resurrection of the body, and life everlasting."

Through Christ we are forgiven. What does that mean for us gathered here today? It's pretty obvious what it means to Jim. Jim has gone on ahead of us. It means everything to Jim. What about us? It shows us that Christ loves us, no matter who we are or what we've done. Christ forgives us and wants us. All he asks us to do is believe in him!

You know, in the last years I've thought a lot about heaven. Wonder what it's like? Would Jim be happy there? What would make Jim happy? What made Jim happy in this life? One of the things that made Jim happy was a new truck!

I was reading last night in Revelation, chapter 21 and 22, about heaven, and it talked of streets of pure gold. It talked about the river of life, and it talked about the tree of life. That made me think back to the time Vicki and the kids and I were going out west. Jim wanted to know where we were going, and when we told him, he said, "You've got to drive through Wind River Canyon." So we went and that was about as close to heaven as my mind could get—a beautiful little highway winding through "sky-high canyon walls" with a river, clear and beautiful, running through the canyon floor, with trees and rocks and sometimes grass, like tiny meadows.

Last night I thought back to Wind River Canyon, and in my imagination, I was there, standing along the road, and the road was like the street in Revelation—gold. And the river and the trees were still and quiet and the grass lush and green, and coming down the road was a truck, a big truck, a new truck. I could see it coming down the road of gold, its paint gleaming, its wheels sparkling. It was immaculate, and I could feel the earth under my feet tremble from the endless power of the engine as the driver clutched through the curves; effortless and beautiful it came.

Across from me is a place to pull over and a walking bridge over the river. The driver stopped there and got out. He didn't notice me, but I knew it was Jim, and he was so happy. He took the walking path that went under the bridge to a little grass area and he sat there and rested; and I heard him say, "*The Lord is my Shepherd, I shall not want. He makes me lie down in green pastures. He leads me beside still waters. He restores my soul. He leads me in the paths of righteousness for his name's sake. Even though I walked through the valley of the shadow of death, I felt no evil, for he was with me. His rod and his staff, they comforted me.*"

"*Why, he could prepare a table before me even in the presence of mine enemies. He anoints my head with oil. My cup overflows. Surely, goodness and mercy will follow me all my days, and I shall dwell in the house of the Lord forever and ever.*"

This, of course, was a dream in my imagination, but it was what my simple mind could grasp as I thought about Jim and what heaven might be like for him. I don't know, of course, but I do know that whatever I can think of in my mind, it must be ten times, a hundred times better than I can imagine. Our God is that great! He can do anything. He can even take our worst fear, death, and turn it into the greatest thing because, you see, it's only in death that we can go on to be with God. Why? Because he loves us that much. He loves Jim, and us, so much that he died that we might live. Let us remember that always. We depend on that grace.

45

"Save Me a Seat, Buzz"

Buzz Davis Funeral

March 21, 2001

My name is Jerry Crane. I am a farmer from the Hartsburg-Emden area. Buzz Davis is my friend.

There are a lot of stories I could tell you about Buzz, just as there are a lot of stories all of you could tell me about him. I am going to share with you a couple of stories, but the main thing, maybe, is not to hear my stories, but to think of your own special times and stories that you exchanged with Buzz, your friend, your father, grandfather, and your husband.

I got to know Buzz in 1977 when he came to a Christian retreat down in our area. After that first retreat, Buzz started going to prison retreats with us, and we had so much fun. We would tell farming and prison stories all the way there and all the way home. You know, if you farm long enough, just about everything is going to happen to you.

There would be six or seven of us riding in that van, and we had the best of times.

I could go on telling those stories, but as always, time doesn't allow. Instead, I want to share something I believe is very important for us all to hear.

I spent last Wednesday, one week ago almost to this very hour, in Gibson City Hospital visiting with Buzz. I was there during the late morning and all afternoon. We both knew it could be our last earthly conversation. We talked about a lot of things—farming and how good he felt Jay, his nephew, was doing. "He is a good farmer," Buzzy said.

Buzzy talked about Kay and how he hated to leave her with all that stuff in the house. He talked about how Kay had taken such good care of him all these years. He talked about Rodney and his family and how Rodney was taking instruction in the church now. He was so happy with the news that Dawn was going to adopt a boy and said, "That will be great!" He said that Melanie and her husband were going to church now.

"I'm really lucky, Jerry. I got to see my children grow up, and I got to see my grandchildren. I know that there will probably be more. I'm really lucky about a lot of things. You know, that first retreat that I went to, Duke Harms talked me into going. He came over one evening in his pick-up truck. Duke told a little about the retreat, and after his little talk, he said, "What do you think? Do you suppose you would like to go?" After some thought, I said, "Yes, I'll try to go."

Buzz told me that Duke skipped and whistled all the way to his truck. "I can still see him going down the lane. You know, Jerry, Duke is a farmer just like me, and he came to talk to me about my faith. I went to that retreat, and at the closing, I knelt in front of a cross. The retreat leader said, 'Buzz, Christ is counting on you.' And I said, 'And I on his Grace.' From that moment on, my life was forever changed. Everything looked different!"

We sat a while pondering his words. Then he said, "I could have done more. I should have done more." A frown came over his face. I searched my mind for something to say, but once more, he broke the silence. "But I remember what you have always said, Jerry. His grace is sufficient for me, I know where I'm going."

Buzz asked, "Would you say a few words at my funeral?"

"Of course," I answered, "but I'm going to tell them not to worry about you."

Buzz agreed. "Jerry, tell me that too!"

And all too quick, it was time to leave. But we had said it all. All that mattered. I read 2 Corinthians 5:1 to him and then we prayed together. He held out his hand, and as I grasped it, we both whispered, "I love you." There we were, two rough-and-tumble farmers. "I love you, Buzz," I said.

As I walked out the door, I turned and saw this physically small farmer all yellow and frail. I felt like I should salute him, but I merely said, "Save me a seat, Buzz."

Kay, Rodney, Dawn, Melanie, family and friends, Buzzy wasn't a very big man in stature, but he was a giant, a giant among men. And God said, *"My grace is sufficient for Buzzy."*

2 Corinthians 5:1—*"we know that if the earthly tent which is our house is torn down, we have a building from God, a house not made with hands, eternal in the heavens."*

46

"The Gift"

Bryan Bergman's Funeral

September 6, 1989

On January 18, 1988, through the miracle of birth, God gave Aaron and Dena Bergman a baby boy. This was their third child. First there were two adorable, petite little girls, Danielle and Jenna, and now a son. They named him Bryan Scott. All too soon it was discovered that Bryan had a problem with his liver, and thus began a long, hard fight by many people to try and save his life. There was no stopping on Aaron and Dena's part. Their families pitched in tirelessly. And the medical team at Wyler Children's Hospital in Chicago did everything possible, and even some things that were impossible, to try and save his precious life. Hundreds of people in the community also got involved praying, and raising money, and lending support.

Last Friday, September 1, after one of the best weeks of Bryan's life, and particularly one of the best days of his life, in the middle of the night,

Bryan got sick. Aaron and Dena took him to Springfield and from there he was transferred by helicopter back to Wyler Hospital in Chicago. He arrived there at 5:30 Saturday morning. At 12:40 p.m. Saturday, September 2, with Aaron and Dena close by, Bryan crossed from this life, his earthly home, into his heavenly home to the waiting arms of his Savior. Bryan was approximately nineteen-and-a-half months old, and in his short life experienced three liver transplants and six other surgeries. It would be true to say that Bryan left this world of doctors and hospitals, of tubes and ventilators, and donors and IC units. But, I believe we must also say that he left this life of parents who loved him and gave themselves for him, a family who loved him, and a community who prayed and supported him.

Aaron and Dena, our hearts go out to you in your grief and your tremendous loss. And yet we thank you for opening up to us and letting us all be a part of your and Bryan's life. It has been and will continue to be a privilege.

The bulletin says this is to be a eulogy. What can you say about a nineteen-month-old little boy? Lots of things. I'd like to pick out a couple of them. Think with me for a minute, Aaron and Dena, and all of us here, what is it that we want more than anything else for our children? Maybe watch them grow up and do things that we are proud of in school? Yes, but that's not the number one thing. See them get married and raise a family and be successful? Yes, that too is good, but still, not number one. Isn't the most important thing in the whole world that we want for our kids, down deep, is for them to get to know God and Christ as their Savior?

Did Bryan know God? I Corinthians 10:13 says, *"God is faithful. He will not suffer you to be tempted above what you are able to stand."* If you are one year old and have had nine operations, and God has promised not to give you more than you can stand, then I have to believe that God was very close to Bryan. "If God was so close," we say, "why didn't he make him well?" We can't answer that. We're not able to comprehend the wisdom of God, but we know his promises are true.

"I will not give more than you can stand," he says. In some childlike way, God had to be very close to Bryan. And Bryan surely knew that comfort and that compassion that only Christ can give. Many times Christ comes through people. Did Bryan know the presence of Christ? I believe there can be no doubt.

The second thing we want for our children after they get to know Christ, is for their lives to be such as to influence others to come closer to Christ. You couldn't have met Bryan without thinking about your own life and letting his smile influence you. One day I talked with Dena when she had Bryan out with the girls, and I thought, "How can he be so pleasant after he's been through so much? What does he know? What if I had to go through what he did?"

Most of us are here today to worship God because of the witness Bryan gave with his life. Bryan's life brought people together, even whole communities to pray and to work together, but most importantly, to reach out and care for one another. Bryan, at least for a short time, caused us to live like we're supposed to live. Yes, Bryan got to know God in the presence of Christ, and Bryan was able to influence us to think about our relationship with Christ.

Bryan lived a full life. Most of us will live many more years and not accomplish one more thing than Bryan did. But what about those whose loss is so great—Aaron and Dena, and your families? Because of your love and relationship with Bryan's Savior, and our Savior, you have received a richness that no one can take away from you. You know what it's like to share life and death with each other, and with the people you met in Chicago at Ronald McDonald House. You have experienced the love of a friend who, less than two weeks ago, buried her own child, yet flew from Florida to be with you to share your loss.

You have been blessed with a sensitivity and a compassion for others that you could have received in no other way. So what are we saying here, that you should be glad all this happened? Not at all. We wish along with you, with all our hearts, it would have been another way. This is where Bryan's Saviour, and our Saviour, comes in. Because Bryan's life and Bryan's death are so much a part of you, Christ is using them to help you to become what he wants you, and all of us, to better become: loving, caring people, sensitive to others' hurts and needs. His wisdom and his compassion will work together for all those who love God.

Bryan Scott Bergman was less than two years old when he died, but yes, he lived a full life. And those of us who knew him, or even knew about him, especially you, Aaron and Dena, are blessed without measure because of him. May God comfort you in your great loss, and may Christ continue to bless you richly as you cherish Bryan's memory always. Please be assured that you will see him again, and that because of Bryan, we are all a little closer to becoming what Christ wants us to become.

47

"A Tryst with the Master"

Thoughts on Death and Heaven

Our devotions that have been assigned to us are coming to an end. The last chapter, which I am about to share with you, chapter eight, is entitled, "A Tryst with the Master."

In the preface of this book, *The Family of the Forgiven*, it is stated that there are countless fine theological books written, but there is a real need for a common man's picture of the Christian life and faith. I wholeheartedly agree and will continue with that concept.

Chapter eight deals with a very important part of our Christian life and that is death, the physical death of his saints.

We would all, I believe, if we would be honest with ourselves, like to forget about this part of our Christian life. In fact, it really doesn't seem a part of the picture of family life. Yet reluctantly, we all know that it most surely is.

Our earthly families are going to break up. They will, and they should. Some will go to college, some will leave to start family units of their own through marriage, and some will leave the family unit, as we know it, through death, most of the time long before we can see why it should be.

I've heard Olaf say, "We are on a pilgrimage," and on this pilgrimage, there is a shifting, one by one, from the restless world to a final home. Where?

God can and does bless our life with each other, under his grace. So much so, that the separation through death becomes a shattering experience, leaving an emptiness that nothing, not even Jesus, is able to fill. Where we laughed together, we now cry alone.

I had always wondered about this. It has been my greatest fear. When I was in the tractor and things were working well and I had time to think, I probably thought about this more than anything. Or at the highest points in my mountaintop experiences, I've always wondered, "What if a member of my family, my household, my wife or my child, what if they should die before me?"

Maybe it won't happen. Maybe I'll go first as an old man or maybe Vicki when she gets to be seventy-five or eighty. Or maybe, just maybe, it wouldn't be as bad as we are afraid of. After all, we have the promises of Jesus. "*I will not give you more than you can stand.*" Jesus will speak to me through his word, through the sacraments, and the church. Maybe it wouldn't be unbearable. After all, we all know that everything we have, including life itself, is a gift from God, and he has a right to call it at any time.

Yet, at a meeting that I was at early this spring, a doctor of psychology, specializing in death and dying at St. John's Hospital in Springfield, told us that in all the things that can happen to a family, nothing can equal the death of a child in terms of stress and anguish. In their tests, they used the number fifty as a measurement of a person's average stress, feelings, and emotions, going up the scale for added worries and burdens and down the scale for good things and happiness and joy. In other words, at fifty, things are average. A wedding day brought joy and would be recorded as somewhere around ten; financial worries raised to seventy; an accident, seventy-five; death of a parent, eighty to eighty-five; death of a spouse, eighty-five to ninety; and death of a child, ninety-five.

Yet, as followers of Jesus, and I mean followers, not discussers, as followers of Jesus, we know that we are not alone. In laughter and tears, he is with us. The one we love who has physically left us is now safe where we, too, know we will one day be.

"In my Father's home are many rooms. If it were not so, I would not have told you that I go to prepare a place for you, and if I go to prepare a place for you, you know that I will come again for you and take you to myself, that where I am there you may be also. Nothing can separate you from my love. Not life, not death. Nothing. You trust me with yourself. Now trust me with those you love. You, too, shall have a tryst with me, but in my time."

Tryst! Do you know what tryst means? My dictionary says: tryst—an appointment to meet at a specified time and place, as one made by lovers; or a meeting by appointment, or an appointed meeting place, as of lovers.

So we say, okay, Lord. But it's hard. I'm telling you, it's not easy to wait. And to understand is sometimes, not sometimes, it is harder. And no matter how much we trust, we must have help, a great deal of help.

Our son, Tim, received a rather bad injury from a wreck, but others have lived much worse off. His recovery was fast. Youth is in his favor, they all said. His attitude was tremendous. He had everything going for him. He had the best surgeon in Springfield. Tim had been brought in at just the right time, when this particular specialist was on call. A head resident that was as sensitive as a mother hen with one chick, and a nurse that in her own words said, "I love him like he was my own." Not even counting the fact that Tim was in a room that totaled $1300 per day to monitor every move and every change. How could he get so sick with me thirty feet away sleeping on the floor in the waiting room, that in a matter of hours his heart literally stopped beating?

Why? Where are the answers? I have gotten two. Number one: what I am talking about right now. Tryst—an appointment to meet at a specific time and place as one made by lovers. Number two: *"Jerry, do not worry or concern yourself. This is not unto death, but for my glory. Tim is alive. Do you believe me? Do you believe what I have told you?"*

That is enough. We praise God that people will be changed for his glory, even though we may never know it, and it will be for *his* glory. And yet, we are able to see changes in not just a few.

We asked if we could see him, his body after he died. They told us, "Of course, he's still your son. He's still a member of your family."

So we go in and sit by his body. And you think, "How can it be so active one minute and so still the next?" You know that he's not the first person on earth to die, and everyone does. Yet you still wonder, "Where is he now?" There's no question that he is not there. That's not really Tim on that cold steel table. Where is he?

Paradise! Jesus himself said to the criminal, *"Today, you will be with me in paradise."* What is paradise? Where is it? What's he doing? The question, no matter how hard you tried not to think about it, kept coming back again and again. *"Where is he?"* Until finally, on your knees, you beg the question to Jesus himself. "Let me see. Please let me see, just a glimpse so I may know that he's okay. Just a glimpse. Just a sign. Just a picture in my mind. Just a word. Please?"

Nothing. At least that's what it seemed. But you know, what God does with me and you and Tim on the other side of this life before the final resurrection is something he has not described for us in any detail. It is his marvelous business. I cannot limit him with my mind or my logic. I lean only on his promises.

This I know. He has promised to take us to himself that where he is we may be also, and that is good enough. We know he can do it. When he called Lazarus out of the tomb after he had been dead for four days, he showed us in a physical way what he can do for all of us and our loved ones in a spiritual way. There is no need to show us again. He is Lord over death!

Let others discuss exactly what is meant by paradise. I'll live by, rest in, and hang on the words *"with me."* Tim is with the Master. What else matters? He is with the Master.

"I am the resurrection and the life. He who believes in me, though he die, yet shall he live. And whosoever believeth in me shall never die." Lest I forget, on Tim's tombstone are the words, *"This is not unto death, but for the glory of God."* Jesus said, *"No one can take out of my hand those whom I love and have called to myself."*

When you have seen a part of yourself move quietly away from this life, then it matters a lot to know that they slip away to the beckoning arms of the waiting Master.

Psalm 116:15 says, *"Precious in the sight of the Lord is the death of His saints."*

Tim was taught in the church the meaning of eternal life, and before he died, he said, "I am not afraid. I think I'm going to die, but if I do, I'll go to heaven."

After learning of Tim's death, a convict (who I had met at a Kogudus Retreat) wrote and said, "I pray today that I may be in heaven before you, and no matter what far corner of heaven I may be in that on the day you arrive, they will call me to be a witness to you and Tim's meeting again."

As we go along life's way and if in your family you see Jesus say to one of them, *"Come with me, now you shall be in my tender care,"* it is a tryst with the Master. Then you and I can better endure the loss and the waiting until we too can be along shortly for the great reunion.

May our Lord and Savior continue to bless us all so richly. Amen.

48

"The Ultimate Healing"

Reaching Out to Those Who Are Grieving

November 3, 1979

John 11:4—*When he heard this, Jesus said, "This sickness will not end in death. No, it is for God's glory so that God's Son may be glorified through it."*

When we found out that we would be a part of this Ultreya, we were eager to do so. We owe our Lord much and want this to be an opportunity that we can glorify him. Also, we feel a very strong affection for all the Cursillo family and all you have done for us, and we hope in some small way, we can return something to you.

Vicki and I live halfway between Peoria and Springfield on Route 121 near Hartsburg. We have four children: Todd, Tim, Tonya, and Tasha. We came to Cursillo in 1975. We don't get back here much because we're involved with people in our area who have attended a retreat like Cursillo called Kogudus. So we feel good to be a part of the Cursillo family and be here with you tonight.

Whenever I hear someone speak, I wonder where he's coming from. What are his beliefs? Why does he say what he says? You may be asking the same thing. I guess what a person says has a lot to do with his faith and how he has arrived at it. I believe all of us get our faith in one of three ways, and I believe, hopefully, in a balance of the three: feeling or what happens in our heart, intellect or what happens in our mind, and our church history and tradition. We need to have a balance.

Sometimes it's easy to get out of balance, especially when something happens that causes much emotion or trauma in your life, or maybe grief. I think we need to remember what our mind gives us, and our church history and tradition that has survived and been handed down through the years by the saints. The church has kept the word itself, the sacraments, the fellowship, and the caring community together. It's stood many tests and survived.

Well, why are we here? One year ago, we buried Tim, our second child. He was fourteen years old, a basketball player, voted most valuable lightweight, and could do a motorcycle wheelie one hundred yards. He was eighth-grade class president and had many friends. He wasn't always as good as he could be and caused Vicki and me to make that trip at least annually to the principal's office, where it always began with, "Tim's not really a bad boy, but . . ."

Before we start our story, we need to go back a little ways. Todd and Tim were on their way to help me in the field when they had an accident. Todd was not hurt, but Tim was. When Vicki got there, she could sense God's promise, *"This is not unto death but for the glory of God."* The ambulance took him to Lincoln and then on to Springfield, St. John's, where they operated. He had internal injuries. Pastor came and said, *"This sickness is not unto death."* We felt this was confirmation.

It must be true. God is going to heal Tim, and this will bring much glory to God.

The operation lasted five hours. Tim was stable, and we could go in. He was hooked up to a conglomeration of tubes and machinery. His care was the best, and he began to improve. In five days, he was off the respirator and sat up. We took pictures and laughed. He continued to improve and got out of intensive care, but then got sick, really sick. He told me to get the nurse. He told Vicki, "I think I'm going to die, but I'm not scared. I know I'll go to heaven." He put aside all that was important for what he knew was all that mattered. Basketball, friends, even Vicki and I could not help him—only Christ.

The next morning, we talked to the nurses. Tim hadn't slept all night, but had been praying. He asked me to pray with him. He seemed to improve, and they sat him up again a few times that weekend. And then, early on Monday morning, I was asleep on the intensive care waiting room floor. Tim had had a bad night. I talked to him. The nurses called the doctor again and told me to call Vicki. She arrived. Tim's heart stopped, but they got it going again. They said they were going to have to operate again. Something had gone wrong inside. We should wait in the hall.

Tim was unconscious, but we knew he would make it . . . this is not unto death.

The nurses were crying. The doctor went by and said, "We'll keep you posted." I called the rest of the family, and we went to the chapel.

Everyone arrived, the family and Pastor. They told Vicki, "Don't give up, remember the verse." The doctor sent word to us that things were not going well. In about fifteen minutes, he came in looking very grave and told us they had lost him. And in my mind went the words, "Lost him?!" Tim's dead, the doctor said so. The verse, our hopes, everything we'd leaned on . . . what happened? Why? Why? I asked the doctor to come and sit with us.

I asked how long ago he died. He said fifteen minutes. We won't pray to bring him back. He wouldn't want to even if he could. The ladies in pastoral care were tremendous. They kind of herded us into a room. There were at least twenty-five people. We prayed, thanked God for Tim's life and death.

We talked with the head resident. "I can't understand it," he said.

We asked if we could see Tim. "Of course," he said, "he's still your son." He took Vicki and me and Todd into a kind of medium-sized room. It had a cement floor with glazed tile. And in the center on a steel table lay Tim, a sheet wrapped around him about to his neck. The sisters had four chairs for us to sit on and asked if we were all right, then graciously left us alone. We sat and talked and touched. It was Tim. How could he be dead? There wasn't a mark on him except, of course, for his incision.

Yet, it wasn't Tim—not really Tim. It was just the shell, an old coat he had thrown down, a body he no longer needed, ready to be buried. Tim wasn't there, he was alive somewhere. We had the visitation at our church and a memorial service. Pastor let me be in charge of the service. It was directed to Tim's friends and was centered on our Savior.

From the time Tim was loaded in the ambulance after the wreck, we had kept the theme, "*To God be the glory.*" We couldn't stop now because he had died. We talked about life forever. Tim was alive. We had asked for physical life for Tim and God gave us more—life.

Afterward, Tim's friends crowded around the casket, and you could hear them say, "Tim isn't there. He must be alive—." Pastor preached the funeral sermon with the same theme. Caring community was never so real. Family and friends were always there. Neighbors plowed the rest of the farm for me. They sat and talked and seemed to understand. Sometimes they just listened.

The word tonight is grief. A part of us is gone physically. We cannot touch or communicate as before. Your heart is laid open. How can it ever heal? You know he's all right, but what about us? All our lives, we had looked forward to high school basketball for Tim. What about those games? What about his room, his motorcycle? We had built a pond. Tim liked to swim. Tim and I built a diving platform together. His basketball from basketball camp, his clothes, this all had to be dealt with. There was an appointment to have the braces on his teeth checked. It would have to be cancelled and we needed to tell them we wouldn't be back. We'd have to get his stuff from school. I guess that's grief. What do we do with it?

We have no set answers on how to deal with grief, either for ourselves, for you, or in helping others with it. We can only give you our experiences and how we feel.

It is hard for us, even as Christians, to help others with their grief. I can only say this: come to us and others who are grieving where we are. We need you, and we also need our grief. Don't take it away from us or ask us to give it up. Let us work through it. Be aggressive in the fact that you can help. Men say they don't need us, or they have other friends, or they want to be alone. Go to them, and see if there is anything you can do, and if they just need your presence, then sit with them. You will know when you get there. They'll tell you if they need to be alone. Don't be offended. We needed people, and we needed to be alone. Of course, you can't say anything that will help, but be there in case they need you.

Jesus comes to us many times through people, and Jesus always comes to us where we are with much patience and love. This was not unto death. Tim is alive, and someday, we will be with him. A person I know in prison wrote when he heard of Tim's death. "I pray that I may die before you," he said, "and on that day when you die, I ask that God would let me be present to see you and Tim when you meet again."

Jesus is good. We still have our grief; it's not going away. I don't want it to. God has allowed it to come into our lives to help us to become more of what he wants us to be, and in the process, has given Tim the best: life with him, the *ultimate healing*.

What is the worst thing that we think can happen to us? It's death, isn't it? Yet our Lord has taken the worst and made it the only way we can get to him. He's taken the worst and made it the best. What a God we have!

Tim is alive, and lest I forget, on his tombstone is printed, "*This is not unto death, but for the glory of*"(John 11:4). And Ephesians 3:20-21 says, "*Now to him who is able to do immeasurably more than all we ask or imagine, according to his power that is at work within us, to him be glory in the church and in Christ Jesus throughout all generations, for ever and ever! Amen.*" Our prayers were answered far more abundantly than we ever considered possible. Tim's body was like an old coat he had thrown down, and then he ran off, leaving it behind. He showed me how precious life is and how to cherish and cling to it and fight for it; yet he showed me some of what it must be like to see something so wonderful, whatever it was he saw, that he was ready to leave this life he cherished so much so he could have it.

I read once about how a baby feels so secure inside the mother and doesn't want to go out into the world, yet when he gets there and sees all the love and all the people waiting for him, he sees how much better it is than where he was.

I wouldn't trade what I've learned, I don't think, for Tim coming back. Tim's okay. He's better off. It would just be for me that I would ask for him back, and I don't want to give up what Tim taught me and did for me. Jesus died for me that I may have life more abundantly. He really is *the greatest*. Thank you for sharing in our grief.

Part VIII

Letters

49. To Alan Lessen 277
50. To Buzz Davis..279

49

Letter to Alan Lessen

May 10, 1998

Dear Alan,

I saw this car the other day and it made me think of our prom in 1956 when Tony Behrends let us borrow his new '56 Chevy convertible. Boy, was he trusting! Vicki helped me dig out some old prom pictures. The colored ones are the '57 prom when we were seniors. I thought I had one with us all in that car riding around Emden after breakfast the next morning, but couldn't find it. I guess memories can be whatever we want to make them, but I remember the '56 prom as the best it could be.

The best part about finding this car and the pictures was it gave me a reason to write and tell you what I've been thinking. It may be important to you and it may not be, but I want you to know it's important to me.

A couple of Sundays ago, I talked to Alice in her Sunday school room and asked her how you were doing. It was the Sunday after you went to the doctor. After she told me what the doctor said, I asked her how she thought you felt. Do you think Alan is scared, angry, or what? She said the only thing you had ever said was you were disappointed.

I thought about that word a lot that day and the next. What does it mean to be really disappointed, and what does that do to a person? That Monday I was looking for some things and found this: *"Disappointment to a noble soul is what cold water is to burning metal; it strengthens, tempers, intensifies, but never destroys it."*

The secret to this, I believe, are the words *"a noble soul."* My dictionary says *"noble"* is having or showing high moral qualities. I've never known a person who has been so dedicated to care for his family and friends, with higher work standards, and without any thought of reward or thanks.

Disappointment to a person who is not a noble soul can be devastating, but I believe to you, Alan, it will bring you to your highest plane. It looks like your days ahead may bring many disappointments, but I know you, my friend, and even though there will be days that bring anger, frustration, and hurt, and even panic, underneath it all lies a *"noble soul"* loved by Christ, and somehow you will be **OKAY**. May God be close to you and your family, Alan.

Your friend,
Jerry

Footnote: Alan Lessen and Jerry were lifelong friends. Alan was suffering from ALS (Lou Gehrig's disease) when Jerry wrote this letter to him. Alan passed away on February 27, 1999, while Jerry was in the hospital recuperating from open-heart surgery.

50

Letter to Buzz Davis

November, 1985

Dear Buzzy,

It's 1:30 a.m. I just got home from the hospital.
They opened you up three times today, Buzzy. They had to massage your heart once. You're bleeding now. You're alive, hanging on by a thread, but the thread is hooked to Christ—I know it. He wants you alive at least tonight or you wouldn't be here. You are alive because Christ wants you alive. I don't know for how long. I hope for a good long time, but that is up to your God.

I'm glad that we met several years ago, Buzz. You have been a *"glad place"* in my heart. You are my friend. If you don't make it, I will cry and feel awful. But I won't feel awful because you don't know that I love you. You know it, and I know that you know it. I'm glad for that, for the chance we had together. It was because of Christ, you know. That's why we're friends.

You have a nice family, Buzz. They love you and you can be proud of them. Kay needs you, but if you don't make it, I know that God will take care of her. I honestly don't know if you will live through this or not. I pray with all my heart you will, yet I must pray, *"Your will be done,"* because he is keeping you alive tonight. I'm sure of that.

May God bless you abundantly as he heals you. He loves you more than you can imagine. I pray that your pain will not be unbearable.

Jerry

(See "Save Me a Seat, Buzz" in Funeral section.)

Part IX

Jerry's Funeral

---

51. "Harvesting for Eternity"—Memories by John Cross
   and Thoughts from Jay Johnson 283
52. Letter from Palestinian Agriculture Relief Committees 287

51

"Harvesting for Eternity"

Jerry Crane's Funeral

January 21, 2006

Jerry died on January 16, 2006, at the age of sixty-four. At his funeral service, John Cross spoke the following words in memory of Jerry, including a story by Jay Johnson:

If I may, I would like to share just a few thoughts with you about the man we all knew and loved, Jerry Crane. Life for Jerry, outside of his loving Christian home, began in a one-room country school called Bethel. This is where Jerry, as a little boy, grew wise and learned in life the simple lessons of obedience, discipline, kindness, and friendship.

I received an email from a friend of Jerry's [Jay Johnson, who was in Bangladesh] this past Thursday and I would like to read it for you:

"*This morning when I got up, I shared with my wife an image that had come to mind. Past Emden, past San Jose, even to the river and beyond, I could see the fields of what looked like corn and soybeans, and it was all fresh and green. Some of it was new growth, some of it was in bloom, and there was some ready for harvest. From where I was, the crop all looked good. I knew it was the seeds that had been planted in the world and each one of those plants were like a person. Then there was this sense that I knew that Jerry and Vicki had planted them all. It had taken a lot of time, but they had put them all there, by hand, over time, and they were growing. I looked around and Jerry was not there. When I asked where Jerry was, the One who spoke to me said with a quiet smile, 'You won't see him anymore, because he is doing a different kind of work now, a work that he enjoys very much.' Then I knew that it was in accordance with the will of the One who sees everything. And I felt good about it all, content in a peaceful sort of way."*

I believe this e-mail speaks volumes about the little boy who grew up on the prairie and learned in life to fling wide the seeds of kindness that were given to him.

Today, across this prairie around Bethel and beyond, fruit from that labor is still seen. The seed was the love of Jesus, and Jerry Crane was a sower for his season! All of us here today have, in some way, been blessed by God through Jerry Crane. Jerry was humble and he understood the urgency of sharing the good news of Jesus Christ!

One of my favorite stories about Jerry was when he first went to a Kogudus retreat. His bag was packed and he and Vicki were sitting in their kitchen. Jerry was not very excited about going. In fact, he was still trying to figure out a good excuse. Then, right on time, his ride pulls up in the yard and Vicki says to Jerry, "Just go, go ahead and go, but whatever you do, don't get involved!"

We all chuckle, because we all know the extent to which, not only Jerry, but also Vicki, got involved. Both Jerry and Vicki, by the grace of God, did not heed that advice. They got involved in loving God and loving God's people! What a team they were!

A friend and I were talking about how much we would miss Jerry. He said none of us may be able to fill Jerry's shoes, but that doesn't mean that we can't walk in his steps. And if we walk in Jerry's steps, we'll be headed in the right direction, because Jerry loved and followed his Lord and Savior, Jesus Christ. Jerry also loved his family and friends very deeply. He invested in people's lives. He cultivated and cherished relationships.

All this week I've been thinking about what Jerry would say to all of us today. What would be his message? Knowing Jerry, I'm pretty sure he'd start by telling a funny story, probably about himself, that would put us all at ease. And he would simply say, "You and I have a great God. Not only does he daily bear our burdens, but he also gives us our salvation!"

52

Letter from Palestinian Agriculture Relief Committees

30 January 2006

Dear Mrs. Vicki Crane and all members of the Crane family:

In the name of the Palestinian Agriculture Relief Committees' administration, employees and rural volunteers, please accept our deep condolences for the passing of our great friend, Mr. Jerry Crane, praying that his soul will rest in heaven peacefully.

The passing of Mr. Jerry Crane was very shocking news to all of us. We still remember the great energy, passion, and devotion our friend Jerry had shared during the Gandhi Tour to the Middle East.

Mr. Crane will always be remembered as the devoted American farmer who exceeded his American borders in search for peace and justice in the Holy Land.

"*I am a farmer: I know how to deal with the weather, how to deal with the drought, but I don't know how to farm when a wall separates me from my land.*" These are Jerry's words during his visit to the Wall in Palestine. He will be cherished in PARC and in Palestine, just as in the US, as a man of justice and peace.

Hope we could be of any help to you and your family in these painful days.

Rest in Peace Jerry. You will be missed.

With our deep condolences,
Dr. Ismail Deiq
Director General
The Palestinian Agriculture Relief Committees
Palestine

Epilogue

Vicki is now a partner with her son in the family farm. Shortly before Jerry's scheduled knee surgery, he and Vicki talked and he said that if something happened to him, he'd like for her to continue farming with Todd. He said, "If you can't, you can't, that's okay, I just wanted you to know how I feel." Vicki feels that conversation has given her purpose and direction in the healing process since her aneurysm and Jerry's death.

She is also an Effective Communication Instructor, President of Kogudus Renewal Ministry in Illinois, and works with the board of Camp Griesheim Christian Retreat Center.

Since Jerry's death, Vicki has had opportunities to speak and share her story on many different occasions. It is her hope that the people whose lives she touches might see that, even in times of greatest loss, there is the opportunity to ask the question, "What can I learn from this that I cannot learn in any other way?"

Compiling this book is Vicki's tribute to Jerry's love and faithfulness to God and to her.

Get Published, Inc!
Thorofare, NJ 08086
17 September 2009
BA2009260